I FEAR NO EVIL
BECAUSE I KNOW MY GOD IS IN CONTROL,
LOVES TRUTH AND JUSTICE, IS ALWAYS WITH
ME AND WILL VANQUISH ALL WHO DEFY MY
RIGHTEOUSNESS AND TRUTH!!!

AND SO, THEREFORE, I WILL NOT BE SILENT! I
WILL SHOUT TO THE WORLD! TO GOD BE THE
VICTORY AND GLORY! AND MAY THAT TRUTH
THAT I HAVE FOUGHT FOR WITH MY BLOOD AND
TEARS AND BROUGHT INTO THE LIGHT,
LINGER MIGHTILY
AND SHAKE THIS WORLD LONG AFTER I AM
GONE FROM THIS EARTH!!!!

WHEN WILL JUSTICE PREVAIL?

PUBLISHED BY ZWORLDNET PUBLISHING INC.
ISBN 978-09712310-6-1 / WWW.ZWORLDNET.COM

ALITA CARTER'S
SENSATIONAL NEW BOOK

WHEN WILL JUSTICE PREVAIL?

AN INSIDER'S VIEW BY A FORMER IRS EMPLOYEE

The Internal Revenue Service:
Acts of Malfeasance, Malevolence and Malice Revealed

PREFACE

I'm pissed and here's why! What are the root causes of problems that exist inside some infamous entities of federal government? I can think of several. Let me start at the beginning. The intended purpose of this endeavor is to bring awareness to the knowingly willful and intentional acts of MALFEASANCE committed within federal government, namely the Internal Revenue Service. Everyone is well aware that wherever injustice rears its ugly head, the threat to justice exists. No matter how minute, an injustice is unjust.

Millions of Americans live in fear of the Internal Revenue Service (hereinafter IRS) because of numerous bad experiences, whereas the **Agency's GESTAPO tactics** were utilized unjustifiably more times than not. However, everyone who works for the IRS is not bad—some are products of the environment in which they work. This is no excuse, it's the brutal truth. In a new poll as reported by ABC News on December 21, 2007, the Transportation Security Administration (TSA) has tied with the IRS as one of the least liked federal agencies. Because of the aforementioned, coupled with governmental waste, fraud and abuse, the one who suffers more and stands a greater risk of loss is the nation's taxpayer, no matter the federal agency!

With much reluctance, I cringe when I consider the number of lives that have been severely impacted, along with the many careers permanently altered due to the level of MALEVOLENCE that's ever present. In a word, INJUSTICES are committed by management officials in violation of law. On an ongoing basis, these acts are committed VOID of regard for established policy, which in itself is unlawful. These comments are not far-fetched. After having lived my nightmare for approximately ten years, I speak from experience. Experience is a brutal teacher. In the final analysis, scars indicate where we've been—they don't have to define who we are or where we're going in this life.

With that being said, problems began for me when I filed my very first grievance against the Agency that eventually led to the filing of an EEO, alleging unfair labor practices, prohibited personnel practices, denial of upward mobility, etc. Prior to having filed complaints, everything was peachy. Needless to say, I saw the telltale signs displayed before me almost instantly, for exercising my protected rights against my employer. To note, this constitutes REPRISAL.

To the outside world, employment within federal government seems to be ideal. On the contrary, SOME managers continuously display an *"arrogance of power"* because they are covered under the Agency's *"umbrella of protection."* Second, they display attitudes of INTREPIDATION based on assurances that no harm will come to them due to their employment status. For the most part, all assurances are met.

Administrative entities that are in place to protect employees from Harassment, Retaliation/Reprisal, Discrimination, etc., fall short of the mark. These entities deviate from long-established policy, practice and procedures that are set forth in the Internal Revenue Code (IRC), Internal Revenue Manual (IRM), the Office of Personnel Management (OPM) etc., just to name a few.

When the administrative process is exhausted and the result is unfavorable for the employee, the only recourse that remains is the pursuit of justice civilly via District Court. Be it known that attorney's who practice Labor Law/Employment Discrimination, are reluctant to accept IRS cases because of the rhetoric and red tape that's involved, citing the Agency's manipulation of the process. Also, some feel that representing IRS employees is a waste of time, regardless of the substantiated allegations.

In other words, the corrupt system is designed for the employee to fail. Inside entities are in *"collusion"* with the Agency. When the need arises for objectivity and non-bias to be exercised, these entities opt on the side of the Agency, despite the underlying fact that documented proof of the Agency's wrongdoing is ever present. Which entity is on the mainline campaigning for the protected rights of the employee? Makes one wonder doesn't it?

Not so many years ago, a current manager (in the department) had the audacity to proclaim, *"you can't win against the Agency because you don't know how to fight!"* He further stated, *"you'll get tired of fighting even before our lawyers start!"* Those words scorched, leaving a gaping hole like hot lava that erupts from Mount Fuji. His insidious comments stuck as if someone had thrown a bowl of hot grits on me. And now after quite some time, his opinions are permanently etched in my memory. Have you ever wanted to respond to an inciteful comment but instead held your peace for the greater good? It's awfully hard to refrain sometimes, but often times we have to grin and bear it.

And, have you ever felt beaten down by an opponent before the first punch is thrown? Everyone is well aware that some first, second and executive level managerial officials operate on double standards. SOME managers feel as though the rules and regulations that we employees are subjected to does not apply to them. For the record, the word *"EMPLOYEE"* refers to all employees, including executives, senior managers and all supervisors.

Management's actions are brazen, above the law and without consequence. For example, when managers willfully and intentionally speak untruths in sworn affidavits, they are not held accountable for committing perjury. Often times than not, they are rewarded via promotions to bigger and better opportunities because the Agency was spared embarrassment by *"ANY MEANS NECESSARY."* Some are offered and/or receive early retirement with full pensions, although they lack the eligibility requirements as determined by the Office of Personnel Management (OPM). In the interim, if lower level employees are found to have committed perjury in an official EEO matter, the end result is removal with no mitigating factors considered whatsoever!

If you secretly polled the employees about the work environment, their immediate supervisors and their personal feelings about the job, you would be surprised to find that the majority opinion represents disturbing and grave levels of dissatisfaction with management. This dissatisfaction is expressed annually in plummeting survey scores prior to fiscal year end. I use the word *"secretly"* because several employees are afraid to speak openly in fear of Harassment, Retaliation/Reprisal, Discrimination, etc., in terms of having their annual appraisals lowered, facing denial of promotional opportunities, some are the recipients of negative write-ups, some names are referred to the Examination Division for the auditing of their personal tax returns (without provocation), some are *"secretly"* reported to the Treasury Inspector General for Tax Administration (hereinafter TIGTA), and some are even talked down to by management, leading to ostracism by their peer group. These things occur as a result of the negative comments that have been stated about them by management to others similarly situated, as well as to other levels of management. Furthermore, a vast number of employees who have risen to the level of *"MANAGER"* lack the Knowledge, Skills, Abilities and Other (KSAO) characteristics that is required for the position in its entirety. This also is a known, proven fact.

So, if my assessment is correct, how is it that certain ineligible employees are continually and consistently promoted into managerial positions? It is my understanding that some employees have gone so far as to contact their *"friends"* in high places for consideration. Notably so, these persons are normally Senior Executive Level managerial officials, as well as Division Chiefs, Area Managers, Territory Managers etc., who have the authority and decision making ability to pull rank, securing the placement/eligibility as requested, hereby circumventing the entire competitive selection process as it relates to promotions. And, the employee even has the audacity to openly brag to others saying, *"I know who I can call. They owe me."* And, more times than not, the employee(s) request is honored, whatever it may be, minute or over the top. What is owed and why?

For example, an employee applied for a promotion out of state, was selected and transferred to that post of duty. After having worked there for a short period of time, this individual submitted documents requesting a *"hardship"* back to Houston. When the request was ignored, the employee placed a call to an *"elite"* acquaintance for assistance. Shortly thereafter, that employee was reassigned back to the Houston office, despite the fact that no vacancies existed. This on its face is unlawful and constitutes *"PERSONAL FAVORITISM."*

I have maintained associations with several individuals who voluntarily stepped down from managerial positions, citing many *"unethical"* directives that were demanded by upper management relating to certain employees. Once you become a manager at IRS, you are not allowed to make independent decisions. Instead, you are expected to follow directives regardless as to whether or not you disagree with that directive. And, you had better not voice your displeasure or you'll be ousted, immediately.

For instance, when a current employee was temporarily promoted to a GS 1101-12 Bankruptcy Specialist (receiving GS 1169-13 pay acting as *"temporary"* manager) in the department, she was advised by a current male manager in Special Procedures Branch hereinafter SPB), *"your role now is to protect management since you've been promoted."* My question: *"Protect management from what?"*

I have accepted this CHALLENGE because the truth must be told. My peace has been held too long. To have a group manager in the office and an acting manager in the same group, both receiving managerial pay in the same pay periods, constitute another violation that's adverse to policy guidelines. However, this action was approved by the Territory Manager in Phoenix. Nevertheless, it's common knowledge that this in fact did occur. Are you wondering what other illegal actions this individual willfully and intentionally committed that has led to waste, fraud and abuse of the system during his reign in this region? If so, keep reading.

After twenty four years of reporting to the same employer day after day, after receiving numerous performance and managerial awards since being hired, even after being looked upon as a leader, I was undervalued. Although I grieved privately, I still felt the need to continue with this ridiculous façade, lying to myself and others about the career that fizzled down to a *"dead-end job"* with no promotional opportunities. That is, if you're an employee in Houston's office of Insolvency. The time for me to *"reinvent"* myself is now.

Although I remain cognizant of the fact that a person should love what they do, I lived a slow death for many years, from having witnessed so many injustices, as well as being *"on the receiving end"* myself. Nevertheless, I refuse to grieve anymore about matters beyond my control, instead concentrating on the things that I can control, somewhat. *Psalms 37:4 states, *"Delight thyself also in the Lord; and he shall give thee the desires of thine heart."* You're probably asking yourself why did I stay around so long and subject myself to these acts? This is a fair question. Here's my response to it.......

The atrocious acts complained about should not occur in government based on the laws that are in place intended to protect employees. Just like the next person, I became complacent and too comfortable. I'm not ashamed to admit that. Had I left ten years ago, I would not have this amazing story to tell. That in itself is a sad commentary. If I hadn't been forced out, I know that I'd still be hanging on—my untapped potential dormant. However, I have finally arrived at the place in life where I can be myself without judgment. I've found my niche.   Often times, we hold on to the things that God himself wants us to let go of. My steps have been ORDERED and I know that this is what he'd have me to do. I say this with much certainty. *"I didn't choose this mission, this mission chose me."* Many times throughout my lifetime, I've heard people exclaim that *"there are two sides to every story."* Although true, there is only one TRUTH. For the simple reason, it stands alone, it is resolute and unwavering.

As it stands, truth is the one thing that will NEVER change with time. In the interim, *"dancing with false prosperity disallows us to walk in truth."* *"To everything there is a season, and a time to every purpose under the heaven; a time to rend, and a time to sew; a time to keep silence, and a time to speak; I said in mine heart, God shall judge the righteous and the wicked; for there is a time there for every purpose and for every work."* *Ecclesiastes 3: 1, 7 and 17*

**LET GOD'S JUSTICE BE DONE ON
EARTH AS IT IS IN HEAVEN!**

CHAPTER I
"IN THE BEGINNING"

How many of you can still recall some of the most memorable times in your lives? For some, it's probably when you graduated from college, perhaps when you gave birth to your first child or maybe when you accepted a marriage proposal, whereas the words *"I do"* exchanged at your wedding ranks in the top ten. There are others who were most happiest when they secured that all important job. It carries greater meaning if you're fortunate enough to still work for that same employer after many years of dedicated service. The date of September 19, 1983, is a date that bears great significance for me.

Not that delivering my own son twenty-five years ago wasn't a momentous occasion; I thought it most urgent to be employed before taking on the responsibility of motherhood. Needless to say, both moments brought about the happiest days for me, and each rank very close to the top of my grading scale.

After graduating from Massey Business College in December 1982, I pounded the pavement daily in search of employment. Although job placement assistance was offered, I refused to wait for the school to place me with a prospective employer. Reason being, anxiety had set in. It has been said that *"the early bird catches the worm"*, so I started out early in attempts to beat others to certain opportunities. Jobs were plentiful then and I knew that sooner or later someone would express an interest in me.

Anyone who knows me knows that I love nice things, especially expensive jewelry and designer handbags. Just like the next person, I have desires also. Therefore, I needed my own cash reserve. And, I'm sure that my father cherished the day when I would no longer raid his pockets in search of greenbacks. This had become common practice with no expectations to ask for spending money. He'd tell me, *"go get what you need, just leave me gas money."* Man, I hit pay dirt! Oh, you know what's been said about payback. I was a daddy's girl, so everyone knew of the special bond we shared. Unfortunately, he's deceased now. I love you dad, "RIP."

On the other hand, my mother is quite different from my father. Where he had a problem saying *"no"* to me, that word doesn't pose a problem for her at all. She's a stern, tough cookie who disallowed me the chance to sleep in, making sure that I made good use of my free time! With that being said, I filled out applications at numerous business establishments in the city and surrounding areas. Although several doors were slammed in my face, that didn't deter me. It was that same rejection that helped me to persevere, despite any adversity I encountered.

Months later, someone mentioned that the Internal Revenue Service was hiring. Immediately, I applied for an administrative position and passed the Civil Service Exam. Yippee!! After receiving the satisfactory results, I patiently waited for a call regarding employment. On September 17, 1983, the call finally came. A female manager identified herself and proceeded to ask, *"Are you still interested in employment with the IRS?"* I excitedly answered yes. She advised me to come to her office two days later for an interview. Prior to the conclusion of our conversation, I thanked her for considering me a viable candidate for employment.

Days later, needless to say, I woke up earlier than usual. In making sure that everything was under control, I prepped for the upcoming interview by making sure that my hair was neat, my clothes were crisp and the shoes that I intended to wear were top notch. Despite what's been said, prospective employers pay very close attention to the shoes you wear. No flip-flops please! Most importantly, my pantyhose were free of *"runs."* No one likes to see so-called professionals with raggedy stockings. I must admit—I looked presentable and was ready to tackle the corporate world after stepping *"outside the box."*

Minutes later, news broadcasts warned drivers of threatening thunderstorms and flooding in Houston and the surrounding areas. So, I left home very early in attempts to avoid bad weather. Anyone who has lived in Houston for any amount of time knows how rapidly water collects in certain areas of town, especially the Southwest side of town. That's where the interview would be conducted.

As I exited the freeway, I noticed several stalled cars along the roads and upon embankments at the intersection of Westpark and Fondren. Because I refused to drive my small car through the water, I was stranded with other drivers waiting for the water to recede. To me, this seemed to take all day. I can't tell you how many times I looked at my watch, fidgeting nervously. After waiting around for about two hours, I thought it best to call my mom to inform her of my whereabouts. Needless to say, I'd already missed the appointed time for my interview by a long shot. Man, I was kicking myself!

Upon hearing my voice, my mom could sense that something had gone awry. She instinctively asked, *"Have you made it there yet?"* I was almost embarrassed to mention that I was stranded. If I knew then what I know now, Metro would have been on speed dial! Naturally, I looked for a detour route but there was none because of the accumulation of water in the surrounding areas where I found myself stranded.

Therefore, I thought it best to not attempt driving through water. Had I tempted fate, I would have had two obligations to satisfy, my mother and the finance company! That is when she advised me that I made the correct decision to wait it out. However, when she realized that my interview hadn't taken place yet, she jokingly stated, *"you're going to get fired even before you're hired."* Actually, this is the exact moment I learned that some things are better left unsaid. I remained silent.

Although taken aback somewhat, I remained steadfast. Reason being, *"what God has for me is for me."* It was my belief that this opportunity would still be available whenever I arrived that day. When the water eventually receded hours later, I successfully reached my destination almost at the close of the business day. Upon reaching the third floor, the manager was waiting at the top of the stairwell to greet me (with a smile), stating that *"she understood the dilemma that I had just faced."* Whew, I thought that she was about to say *"Ms. Carter, your services are not needed."* She did not say that. Little does she know, I could have kissed her. For the simple reason, her approach helped make me feel at ease, although my stomach was in knots.

At that moment, she directed me to Personnel for fingerprinting instead, whereas on September 19, 1983, I was hired as a Clerk-Typist (GS 322-3). After serving an eighteen month probationary period, I was retained in the Service as a permanent employee.

Anytime a person starts out on a new mission, it's interesting and exciting. I was elated to be affiliated with a well-known entity as the IRS. Or at least I thought. After reporting to duty, the manager introduced me to my coworkers, some of whom I still have close associations with today, after all of these years. Afterwards, she walked me through the work area and explained the job duties. Man, I thought that I was somebody because this was a prestigious organization.

At the time of my appointment to federal service, I was only twenty one years of age. The job required that I have my own desk, typewriter and access to the computer. The only thing left to do was impress my manager daily, by producing quality work that exceeded company expectations.

In May 1984, the department previously known as Office Branch changed to Automated Collection System (hereinafter ACS), whereas the department consisted of Office Collection Representatives, Tax Examiners, etc. The system was revamped, allowing the collection process to flow smoothly, providing the availability to reach more customers. Because I did not have the experience required for either position, I familiarized myself with the job by assisting coworkers with the collection of computer printouts from Integrated Data Retrieval System (IDRS) to help resolve their cases.

After watching and listening to this process for several years, I found the job to be somewhat intimidating. On a daily basis, I would overhear conversations between IRS personnel and the taxpayer that I considered to be highly inappropriate and offensive. I make reference to instances where IRS personnel would verbally chastise and belittle the taxpayer, for whatever reason. What's with the *"Kinder, Friendlier IRS?"*

Despite my earlier apprehension, in 1987 I applied for the position of Tax Examiner and was promoted to a GS 592/4-7.

My tour of duty was from 4:30 p.m. to 1:15 a.m. daily. I loved this tour because it provided an opportunity to stay home with my two small children, whereas their father worked days and stayed home with them at night. Yippee, no paid babysitter! I also loved this shift because it came with a few more incentives. Most importantly, I worked with a professional manager, we had a small group and the employees respected one another, regardless of any varying differences of opinion, etc. These things are critical to a group's success.

CHAPTER II

Shortly thereafter, I became more comfortable with the required job duties. Actually, I had expressed an interest in being a Tax Examiner years before I applied for the position. As I performed my assigned duties, if I ever found myself to be unsure about what actions to take on a particular case, my manager was readily available and willing to offer assistance. He would not openly ridicule me and lower my evaluative appraisals for not having known how to proceed. Instead, he coached and developed his employees, advising us that *"it was human nature to feel uncertain in different situations, and/or to make honest mistakes."*

I have always declared that a manager's role is to prepare his/her employees for advancement towards better opportunities, with greater emphasis placed on promotions. Aside from that, if certain employees express interests in temporary *"details"* to other departments, those requests often times are denied, depending upon who you are and whether or not you're liked by management. In the interim, if you have opposed management for whatever reason or if you have participated in the complaints process, either through EEO/National Treasury Employees Union (hereinafter NTEU), you may as well hang it up, because it's a *"well known fact Jack"* that your career dies! To save yourself from embarrassment, you may as well not apply for job vacancies.

Simply put, one phone call from management opposing your consideration for an announced promotional opportunity happens more often than I care to admit. To compound matters, while you're patiently awaiting notification regarding eligibility, your paperwork finds its way to *"file thirteen."* As a form of punishment, an employees' intent to advance within the organization is stymied for the duration. Certain names are placed in the bottom of the barrel and intentionally passed over, time and time again, as instructed by management. Once again, these acts constitute REPRISAL.

Some employees have applied for promotions, were identified as best qualified via personnel, they advanced to the interview process but were notified that the vacancy had closed as non-select. How could that be if each of the candidates met and exceeded the required qualifications for consideration in this prospective promotional opportunity?

I can think of three reasons this occurred. First, management did not approve of and/or disliked specific candidates on the promotion certificate. Second, the preferred candidate(s) on the promotion certificate didn't perform well enough during the interview process. Third, maybe management's personal favorite did not apply. So, before management risked selection, they arbitrarily chose cancellation instead. Please don't insult my intelligence by mentioning the *"budget!"* If a budget issue existed, why announce the vacancy?!

Therefore, who comes out on the losing end? The employee, always. It stands to reason that if no one met eligibility requirements, personnel would not have forwarded a selection certificate to the selecting official. So much for fairness and equality huh? Furthermore, one is led to believe that a selection is imminent.

With non-selection of a candidate, employees grow weary and refuse to express interests in future opportunities. Non-selection affords privileged employees the opportunity to hone-up on their interview techniques in preparations for upcoming vacancies. This go-around, the golden child will have applied, whereas in all likelihood the interview/selection process will flow more smoothly, for management that is.

Senior executive level management officials have their noses in the sand, refusing to admit to themselves and others that these and many more discriminant acts exist, having the audacity to compare this Agency to other large organizations. A female senior executive level official stated to an EEO Counselor during questioning that, *"acts of discrimination just doesn't happen here."* She further states, *"if it's found that a manager has violated policy, that/those individuals will be dealt with accordingly."* **Yeah right!**

Exactly what is it that sets IRS management above committing acts of reprisal? Surely, it's not adherence to policy. We employees are well aware that this Agency has laughed at established policy for years, insisting on and getting by doing things their way, regardless of law or being recipients of the consequences that should follow.

If her statement has any validity, why then in October 2006 was an employee in the Houston office of Special Procedures Branch (SPB/Insolvency) victorious in winning her DISCRIMINATION complaint against the Agency? The Agency filed a request for Reconsideration to the Administrative Judges' findings that resulted in their own request being DENIED and the ruling in complainants' favor UPHELD. The complaint alleged what else? REPRISAL, HOSTILE WORKING ENVIRONMENT, WORKING CONDITIONS, EVALUATIONS, etc., as well as several other violating acts. Correct me if I'm wrong, but if these acts are nonexistent, how could this employee have secured a favorable ruling? So, for Agency management to voice that these are only *"mere"* allegations is a farce!

What's treacherous is that the named management officials HAVE NOT been dealt with whatsoever. To date, these same managers still occupy the positions that they held prior to several complaints being filed, and subsequent its findings of discrimination against an employee in the Houston office of Insolvency. Second, some have been promoted subsequent the discrimination ruling. What's ludicrous is, these same managers are appointed to act in higher graded temporary positions in the absence of their supervisors, often times receiving exorbitant pay increases, depending upon time served.

Question: *"When does RRA98 provisions come into play?"* These provisions are being misapplied for some privileged employees! The infractions surrounding these findings has led to Agency management's culpability.

Again, this is a prime example of *"double standards"* based on employee status. By ignoring the obvious, her biased comments scream perjury and its contents oozes from a total lack of credence! A current male manager in the department has vehemently exclaimed that *"he is not going anywhere!"* Further saying, *"his own manager will go down before he does!"* What he fails to realize is that in the grand scheme of things, he is and always will be the fall guy, scrambling for the crumbs that's thrown in his direction. What's absolutely unfortunate about his off the wall sentiments is that in his mind, he actually believes what he says.

There's a lot to be said about managers who look for the best in his/her employees, in terms of helping them to excel and reach greater heights within the organization. And, then you have some managers who have gone above and beyond the call of duty to ensure that certain employees do not advance at all, definitely not at/above their own level, even if the employees' qualifications are exemplary. That's what's commonly referred to as *"crabs in a bucket."* The crabs can't get out and they don't want to stay in.

In relation to crabs, why would I want to stay in the same old rut year after year, knowing that some things never change? *"The ones who are committing the wrongs are the same ones who consistently make adverse business decisions!"* I agree that employees should be rewarded for exceeding the norm and others should be reprimanded for failing to meet business objectives. However, reprimands should NOT be grade based nor should the law be misapplied or disregarded because of one's position of authority within federal government! From the Commissioner of IRS, to senior executive level management, to supervisors/subordinates, any/all reprimands should be applied accordingly based on penalty guidelines.

In management's efforts to express discontent, no employee deserves to be ridiculed based on likes or dislikes. Everyone is valued by someone, that's the good thing. Management has failed to realize that no two employees are the same. For instance, some are laid back and accepting, whereas others are tenacious and less accepting but committed to producing a quality work product daily. Just because an employee is not always in agreement, that employee should not be singled out and mistreated for having a difference of opinion. And, they should not be ridiculed for committing honest, inadvertent mistakes. Despite what's been echoed in the department by someone particular, *"no one person knows everything."* I don't ever recall working with anyone in the office who remotely resembles EINSTEIN!

To note, the employees who are quiet, low-keyed and always in agreement with management are the ones to be feared. They absolutely ABHOR management the most, silently causing destruction and dissension across territories amongst a secret sorority who know the real deal! Funny isn't it? What's funny is that management actually considers these individuals to be allies because of their unsuspecting nature. Just like looking at a photograph, smiles don't constitute happiness. Things aren't always as they seem.

Want to know something else funny? These same employees display two faces in managements' presence due to cowardice and fear of reprisal if they express their true feelings, verbally and/or implied. In a lot of instances, these employees tend to be much more dangerous than the supervisors they report to. However, management is under the impression that they're liked by some. As soon as the managers' back is turned, they become the objects of ridicule by the ones they favor via exception and exemption.

A male manager in the department at the time lamented, *"We (employees) don't know how to play the game."* What game? Although it's a known fact that he's full of games, the workplace is no place for them. To have your career and livelihood jeopardized is not funny one bit! Most importantly, just because you're a manager, that does not give you the right to criticize others. Your title does not set you above anyone. Despite all of the documented acts of injustices committed, GOD is a GOD of JUSTICE. One day, we each will have to give an account for every word, deed or wrongful act committed. The good thing is, it's never too late for redemption.

CHAPTER III

In 1991, my personal relationship with my children's father ended. For the record, we never married one another. Because we dated for several years and filed independent of each other, his social security number was a fixture in my memory. As any parent can attest to, it's hard raising a family on one income, although *"both"* parents are gainfully employed. Sometime thereafter, I filed for child support but needed contact information for the processing of my case. Out of desperation one day, I entered his social security number into the computer and found a bonanza of information.

This avenue proved successful, because each time he was about to be served, he'd quit his job(s) to elude the process servers in Dallas. Finally, there was no need to be evasive any longer. However, before he could be served one last time before the case was about to be forwarded to the proper authorities, he contacted my caseworker and agreed to appear in her office once the date was set.

I was contacted and briefed on what transpired during conversation with this person. She asked, *"Ms. Carter will you be available to meet this upcoming Saturday? We may need to establish paternity on the alleged father and the children."* I agreed to be present, but I said to her, *"the need to establish paternity is not going to be an issue in this matter. Allow me to save the State of Texas a few dollars. When you see the Respondent, all of this will become evident because his children favor him so much, I guarantee that he will not deny the obvious. Furthermore, he's fully aware of my position as the Petitioner!"*

When he appeared, once my caseworker looked at him/them, she said, *"Have a seat please. I'll have you out of here momentarily, after the appropriate documents are signed and both parties receive their copies accordingly."* What did I tell you? Establishing paternity, no need! She and I chuckled amongst ourselves once his back was turned.

Before their father appeared, my three year old daughter was sitting in my lap, and my four year old son (at that time) was being rambunctious as usual. Once they heard his voice, I instantly became someone whom they didn't recognize anymore. I was awestruck. They hadn't heard from him or seen him in several months to years, but they still knew him to be *"daddy."* Moments later, the kids left the office with him, holding hands and swinging their miniature arms as a gesture that they were pleased to be in his space after the long hiatus.

Because I unwittingly had no other recourse but to become the primary caretaker to a great extent earlier on, my feelings were hurt somewhat, although I was elated for them at the same time. You see, that encounter afforded my babies the opportunity to spend much needed time with not only their father, but a male figure at best. A father's role is vital. Role models are found in the home, and it should start with a firm foundation. I grew up with a father in the household. Someone who laughed, played with and hugged me on a daily basis. Why would I want anything less for my offspring?

In realizing that sometimes there are extenuating circumstances, why penalize our children because their parents are at odds with one another? This experience taught me how resilient and endearing children are, no matter their age or gender. Nevertheless, they are God's gifts to us, with expectations to be loved and cared for constantly and consistently. These are requirements that anyone who considers themselves a parent shouldn't mind honoring.

No matter how we look, no matter our size, no matter our mannerisms, our children love us unconditionally. Why aren't our feelings towards them reciprocal in most instances? To be loved and accepted for who you are, your individuality and what you bring to the table is an absolutely beautiful thing.

Aside from the mundane, don't think for one minute I escaped punishment. For all intended purposes, I served a fourteen (calendar) day suspension (from May 1- May 14, 1995), after a security investigation was conducted. When I was summoned upstairs for questioning, I was probably more frightened than I had ever been in my life! At that time, I had been an employee with the Service for twelve years and had never experienced anything so traumatic. No one likes to be summoned by management, let alone being called to appear upstairs in the penthouse.

At the onset, management advised me that the suspension had to occur because I used the computer for personal gain. When questioned about this access, I accepted responsibility and did not deny involvement. How can you possibly deny involvement when the evidence is slapping you in the face? Although any recommendation other than an admonishment was harsh for a first offense, I was forthright and accepted this punishment as the adult I held myself out to be. Furthermore, NTEU didn't object to the Agency's proposal to suspend.

Management has deemed this infraction as an adverse action. According to the National Agreement between the IRS and NTEU, an adverse action is defined as: a removal; a suspension for *MORE* than fourteen (14) calendar days; a reduction in grade; a reduction in pay; and a furlough of thirty (30) calendar days or less of a full time employee. Remember, this incident occurred over thirteen years ago. Should I still be penalized or would you logically think the statute has expired? Or does statute matter? Question: *"Is this or isn't this an adverse action?"* If I am not mistaken, the only time that statute does not apply is in murder cases. I vehemently admit that I did not kill anyone, so why is this considered a first offense?

When criminals are arrested, charged and tried through the penal system, after being released back into society, their debt(s) are considered paid. Sometimes their records are expunged. This is an example of the games that's played within the organization that eventually cause detriment to the lives and careers of impacted employees. Problem is, the intent is for the employee to not figure out that they're about to get slam dunked! After serving the suspension, I relocated to the downtown office, accepting a position as Tax Technician/Tax Examiner in SPB, prior to the phase out of ACS. Years later, I inquired about and expressed an interest in the position of Revenue Officer and what that particular job entailed because that was the wave of the future, requiring employees to personally interact with customers via field visits to residences and businesses regarding their respective tax obligations.

When I heard horror stories about how taxpayers would react when the *"IRS"* knocked on their doors, my interest in this position faded. I was informed that some employees had buckets of water thrown on them; some were attacked by family pets and even threatened with their very lives! After hearing these things, I thought it best that I remain in the office. Not that I am a scary person, it's just that when you know what's best, it's better not to tempt fate. One cannot exactly fault the taxpayer though. No one likes having things taken from them, let's be honest.

You have to remember, that prior to the passage of law referred to as RRA98, some IRS representatives were notorious for committing unlawful acts against America's taxpayers. Short of some committing suicide, some taxpayer(s) pulled out all stops to respectively protect what they considered to be theirs. Unfortunately, I received calls from taxpayers advising me that, *"they were going to commit suicide, due to the fact that they had become overwhelmed in dealing with anyone at the IRS period!"* Quite naturally, these sorts of calls unnerved me and I did everything that I could to keep the lines of communication open.

Although I have never professed to be a psychologist, my advice was, *"for every problem there's a solution and I was there to help no matter how long it took."* Actually, I honestly believe they only wanted someone to listen in their times of despair. just think how lonely one feels to not have someone pay attention to your plight. Where would we be if there was no one to listen? I cannot fathom that thought.

For those of you who have ever contemplated completing suicide, take a moment to think about what you'll be leaving behind. Although it's a fact that if you follow through with your plan to end things, your problems will cease to exist. However, the grief created for your loved ones will be insurmountable. Remember, problems are temporary—death is absolute. Whatever the case may be, God's promise is that *"this too shall pass."* Believe it. I confess today that the Devil is a liar!

How would you like to work day in and day out all of your life to acquire the *"American dream"*, just to have it taken from you in the blink of an eye? Sometimes, it's hard for a person to start over. This is no laughing matter. To have these things happen is disheartening. As a reminder, an ounce of empathy is priceless.

CHAPTER IV

After returning to duty weeks later, I was anxious to quickly learn everything about this new position, delving into my work in attempts to forget what I had experienced. When people say that change is good, I'll always agree. Familiarizing myself with research afforded me the opportunity to learn at my own pace, due to the fact that I honestly don't like having to ask questions of others. And, some employees don't like being bothered with having to respond to them. It's no secret, not everyone has your best interest at heart.

Although I consider myself to be the consummate team player, I have been told that *"I can't expect everyone to be like me."* Some employees have resigned themselves to function inside of their own cocoons, preferring not to interact with others. I'm baffled. How are these same employees exceeding in Critical Element (1): Employee Satisfaction-Employee Contribution, when they do not work and play well with others, according to the mandated performance plan?

As I continued to familiarize myself with the required job duties of this new and somewhat challenging position, I was informed that prior to my arrival, Caucasian managers/employees and Hispanic employees, openly referred to and addressed the African American employees as NIGGERS! They actually used the "N" word. How insulting! For the record, one shouldn't be so quick to cite that word without knowing its exact meaning. I've always believed in the one thing that makes our nation great is something commonly referred to as diversity. We would live in a backwards society if everyone looked alike and had the same thought processes. Each of us should be valued for what we bring to the table, for it's our differences that make us alike in so many ways.

When the employees brought this to the attention of the Caucasian Chief of SPB, his response was *"what do you expect me to do about it?"* I have no reason to express disbelief, because when I reported to the downtown office, a male Caucasian management official displayed an act of repudiation for me as we were introduced. His one comment was, *"I have heard about you!"* For a moment there, I thought I had bubonic plague because he absolutely refused to shake my hand. (He was unaware that I had heard about him also, but to reveal this would have been pointless)!

His ignorance and lack of professionalism did not dissuade me one bit from reaching my intended purpose, although common sense dictated that I perform above the level of fully successful. From that moment on, my actions and movements would be monitored. '

Days later, our group manager cleared his office, signed his exit papers and left without a goodbye to anyone. The buzz around coffee pots is he mailed his credentials back to the office versus hand delivering them. That's when you know you've had enough! Again, this manager wasn't allowed to make independent decisions where his employees were concerned. Several of my peers wandered in the wilderness for days, contemplating who the replacement would be. Common sense dictates that one should appreciate what they have—you don't know what you'll end up with! And oh boy, we were all headed for the ride of our lives! It's been stated that not everyone is cutout to be a manager. I agree. Nevertheless, everyone deserves the opportunity if their little heart desires.

On the flip side, one should have the common courtesy and decency to admit failure when the situation permits. There are managers who are blind to the truth, actually believing that they are exceeding expectations based on the IRS's mission. ***Yes, it's true that some are in fact exceeding expectations but they're not written anyway according to policy. Who are you kidding? Shucks, IRS management officials abide by their own set of rules via exemption from national policy and its regulations***. actually, I'm not sure if some of them even know what the IRS Mission Statement says.

For instance, it was stated that when our group manager submitted employee performance appraisals to his superior for review, he was advised to arbitrarily lower certain employee appraisals without provocation and warrant, based on his personal feeling towards that/those employees, coupled with the race factor, African American. So, instead of being openly defiant and insubordinate, our Hispanic group manager opted out via retirement. Weeks later, a female individual reported to the group as his replacement. From the onset of her arrival she demanded perfection from us. Although no system is perfect, why does management expect perfection from its employees?! Didn't I say earlier that managers should lead by example?

What's odd is that this female manager would always complement me on the quality work that I produced, but at the same time made me feel as though the quantity of work produced was minimal. I thought the IRS did not operate on a quota based system? One day I entered her office and asked permission to attend an offsite creditor's meeting with my peer, a Chapter 13 Bankruptcy Specialist. Since I was only a Technician, this seemed to be a good idea, as it relates to other areas/aspects of bankruptcy, leading to advancement. My manager responded by saying, *"Sure Alita that's fine, as long as you are current with your work."* I was current and opted to attend the meeting days later, Friday of the same week. However, I had not been instructed to advise anyone of my whereabouts prior to leaving the building.

My manager was off that Friday but left one of her "cronies" in charge as acting manager. Coincidentally, when I reported to the group, this employee and I were team members. Because she was higher-graded, my desk became the dumping ground for cases that she refused to resolve independently. That was her way of taking advantage of the *"new kid on the block."* Lo and behold, it did not take long for me figure out that there was a *"fly in the ointment."* Although I was new to the department, I was not an amateur in the Service.

From that moment on, my relationship with this individual was strained as a result of me letting her know that I was aware of her intentions. Because of her disdain for me, she informed our group manager that I had been away from my workstation practically all y goofing off somewhere. Due to her accusatory nature, I learned firsthand how some people let authority go to their heads! Then again, I wouldn't consider a twenty-four hour acting assignment to be relatively important.

Common sense dictates that before a person accuses someone of wrongdoing, one should conduct an investigation beforehand, so as to circumvent any hard feelings when those accusations prove false. All weekend I pondered about how I'd handle the confrontation with management, sensing that something unfortunate would transpire. When my manager arrived to work the following Monday, she immediately and nastily summoned me to her office via telephone.

As I entered, I noticed her doing the usual, primping in the mirror applying makeup, looking like a reject top model. Despite what people believe, it's a known fact that internal beauty is more important than external beauty. In saying so, the shell is going to crack regardless of the numerous attempts to evade the inevitable by concealing outward flaws. What's preserved internally remains the same year after year because it's genuine and not superficial.

Before affording me the opportunity to say good morning, my manager angrily said, *"Where were you on Friday Alita?"* As she salivated at this faceoff, it was quite clear that greeting me professionally wasn't at the top of her agenda. I informed my manager that I was in attendance at the Creditor's Meeting. Her response was, *"why are you attending Chapter 13 meetings and you're only a Technician?"* Ok, what's wrong with this picture? She angrily said, *'I did not approve your leaving the office!"* Now she has selective memory. I've lived long enough to know that people remember what they want to remember.

At that moment, the ounce of trust that I had for her became transitory because she had stated an untruth, we both knew. I can deal with a lot of things, different personalities and such, but falsehood is not one of them! Why would I defy her by leaving the office without her approval? If that was my intent, why would I ask permission? Although I received stellar performance ratings under her tutelage, her treatment was unfair. Subsequent that encounter, if I returned from lunch minutes late, she'd leave very nasty inflammatory notes in my chair to let me know that she had been there. During discussions about this matter, I kindly asked that she please afford me the opportunity to report my leave before attacking me and literally calling me a thief! My manager's actions were cold, calculating and callous at best.

Without a doubt her actions were disparate. I never knew her to place notes in the chairs of others. That's totally unfair. Then again people say that life is not fair. She supervised individuals who abused the liberal leave policy by not reporting to work timely, some abused their lunch and break periods by staying longer than the allotted times, some stole leave by not reporting absences on their timesheets, and some intentionally refused to call her office to request annual/sick leave.

Nevertheless, all of these policy violations were accepted by her and often times committed by the same employee(s) who's considered to be her friends. She was aware of everything that she's been accused of and responsible for approving/denying leave requests prior to signing timesheets. Better yet, she made no effort to reprimand these employees. Could it be she favored them above the rest? Just when you think no one's watching, someone is. Always.

CHAPTER V

When my manager was upset with me, she'd avoid eye contact with me. However, her body language alone spoke volumes in terms of what she could not verbalize, that is if she intended to remain the professional that she held herself out to be. I distinctly recall having a conversation with my peer one morning regarding a work-related issue when this manager angrily approached, demanding that we take our conversation outside. She was infuriated, to say the least. The individual/coworker that I conversed with had recently filed a grievance against her. So had I.

To reiterate, anytime this manager witnessed employees conversing in the work area, for some strange reason she'd become antsy and unwired, but not enough to demand from others what was expected of me. When the Union steward questioned her about our allegations, she stated that *"she does not have a problem with my work, only my attitude."* Why did she place so much focus on me? I thought that to be odd because each of us had shown her a great deal more respect than she had earned! She was hell-bent on reprimanding me, but her actions were unwarranted. Nevertheless, I did not respond to her nasty comment, allowing the Union representative to intercede on my behalf.

My manager did not like the fact that I stood up for myself by opposing management's wrongdoing. Eventually, we worked things out and the issue(s) were resolved amicably. Or at least I thought.

Shortly thereafter she was reassigned to another office, whereas a male manager replaced her. Prior to his arrival, he attended a closed door briefing with the outgoing manager in her office. It doesn't take a rocket scientist to figure out who/what was being discussed! When he passed my workstation, a coworker was standing there as we conversed. The managers entered the office and closed the door abruptly. Moments later, he opened the door several times peeping to see if my visitor was still there. This is a subtle form of intimidation that managers utilize against employees to exert authority. At the conclusion of the day, he approached and asked *"Ms. Carter, will you be working tomorrow?"* My response was yes. He asked that I stop in to see him as soon as I arrived.

When I reported to work the following day, I signed onto my computer as usual to take care of a few minor details before I approached his door. I guess I was taking too long because he entered my workstation to remind me that I had an appointment, angrily saying, *"I'm waiting Carter!"* Why are men so impatient? He didn't even say good morning. How rude! After securing my computer, I approached my manager's office as he motioned for me to come in and take a seat. I sat in the chair nearest the door, just in case the need arose for a quick exit. Our eyes met, he smiled and immediately opened up by advising me to limit my visitors. He said, *"Carter you're a social magnet. Several employees congregate in your work area, visiting must be halted to a minimum."*

As he spoke, I looked at him in amazement, maintaining my composure until he'd finished with his unsolicited criticism. Ok, now he's a psychic. In my honest opinion, he could not have arrived at that assessment unless he had been told that by someone in particular. Reason being, we did not know one another professionally or personally. That morning would be his first full day reporting to the department. And, he had only witnessed one visitor the day before. So, when did I become a social magnet?

I knew who the real culprit was. I'd gotten a bad *"wrap"* based on the biased comments that had been stated to him by his colleague, the departing manager. I'll be the first to admit that yes, I did have visitors from time to time, but no more than the next employee. Only difference, my movements/visitors were being monitored, which in itself is disparate. It is my contention, if you can show me one employee who does not have visitors regularly, or an employee who does not visit others regularly, I'll eat glass!

Quite naturally, nothing about this was outside the norm. You have to remember that we all worked together for twenty plus years and had formed close relationships. Visitations were to be expected with boundaries we all adhered to. That meeting could have turned out quite differently depending on how I handled the information that was filtered down to me by this incoming manager. However, I respected the position. Although he tried to come down hard on me, it didn't take me long to realize that that wasn't his nature. In other words, he made a good first impression. Why fault me though because I'm popular?

To the dismay of some, there are a couple of employees within the department who actually love me unconditionally. When I mentioned these things to him, he said *"Get off your high horse Carter and get back to work."* Not only was he my manager, sometime thereafter his opinion(s) became valuable. As a reminder, *"people will **sometimes** forget what you said, they will **sometimes** forget what you did to them, but they will NEVER forget how you made them feel, good or bad."* Amen.

Often times, managers abuse their positions of authority by placing their feet on the throats of some, in attempts to prove who has authority. This individual was the total opposite. From that moment, he earned respect from me. You see, some people are under the impression that respect comes automatically. For the record, respect is earned and it's a two-way street. In order to get respect, you must give it. In the alternative, be willing to accept *"whatever comes what may."* This manager stressed that the objective was for employees to produce a quality work product for the organization on an ongoing basis. Anything less was unacceptable and he held ALL of us accountable for our assigned inventories. Although he was stern, we were a happy group.

I have heard him exclaim so many times, *"If they give me what I need, I'll give them what they need. It's a give and take situation."* His rationale was *"people come first, anything else is secondary."* He wasn't typical because he didn't feed on which employee(s) to harass, misuse and abuse on any given day. Reason being, he liked people and from what I witnessed, they liked him too. Aside from that, in order to love others, you must first love self. That's an absolute must.

This manager set the tone and his examples have not and cannot be duplicated. I have witnessed him become visibly upset when another manager would accuse one of his employees of wrongdoing, unjustifiably. He defended his employees at all costs. Mainly because everyone knew that his employees met/exceeded every deadline that confronted us, often times taking on additional assignments.

During an executive meeting with departmental heads, one of his colleagues openly accused him of *"letting Alita get away with murder."* According to him, he defended me once more. I believe that. His response to this colleague was, *"Anytime you want to review her work, feel free."* Because he took that stance, rumors surfaced that we were sleeping together. Nothing could be farther from the truth. Instead of falsely accusing employees of fraternization on the job, someone should remind Agency management officials that *"happy employees are productive employees."* For the record, some men and some women can be friends without taking things to the next level. A very wise man told me that *"when friends sleep together, the relationship changes."* Who am I to disagree? To date, this VIP is still my BFF......

After working with this manager for only a short period of time, I found his management style to be like none that I had ever experienced, with the exception of a former female manager who saw fit to retain me in the Service after months of serving in a temporary clerical position many years earlier. And, I still hold her in high regard. If there's one word that I'd use to describe their management style, that word overwhelmingly would be *"FAIR."* What more can an employee ask for?

CHAPTER VI

Unfortunately, he was reassigned back to the Gessner office, for whatever reason and the prior female manager returned as his replacement. This time she came back with a vengeance and it infuriated her when his name was mentioned. One day we attended a group meeting to discuss work procedures. The groups' secretary innocently offered suggestions as to how certain work processes flowed smoothly under the former manager's leadership. This female manager shouted, *"I'm tired of hearing about this man! There's a new SHERIFF in town, get used to it!"*

We were all stunned and hush mouthed, asking ourselves *"what was in her granola bar this morning?"* It was as if she was about to spit nails at the group! If this were to happen, I wanted to be out of harm's way. In no uncertain terms, she was going to be *"Queen Bee"* whether or not we disagreed with her perception of herself.

Based on her behavior, this is the number one reason some employees refuse to work for female bosses with *"alpha male egos."* (Don't ask me to state the other obvious reasons). Therefore, when professional females shatter the *"glass ceiling"*, it's incumbent upon other females to have each other's backs. The struggle to rise to prominence in a male oriented culture is tough enough because the dominoes are already stacked against us. It's as if some women forget that they're wearing dresses not suspenders. Then again, if one is confident in its own shell, other females and/or males wouldn't pose a threat whatsoever. Why do women feel that they have something to prove? Just think, treating employees how you'd like to be treated is a beautiful thing.

Initially, when the former male individual reported to the department as group manager, a new department Chief (Caucasian male) reported as well. To my surprise, I liked him right away because he was a jokester and easy to talk to. His open door policy was just that. He always took time from his busy schedule to address employee concerns. Quite naturally, I had heard some unsavory things about him from field employees, but did not allow the negativity to cloud my judgment.

After getting to know him for myself, I appreciate the fact that he respects employees who actually earn their salaries. If an employees' work was lackluster, you knew what to expect. What's funny is that no employee considers their work to be lackluster. *"The ones who fall behind constantly and consistently are the ones who snub their noses at those employees who exhibit ethics and integrity in the workplace daily."*

On one other occasion, our group was gathering for a meeting in the conference room. Feeling the need to impress her boss, our manager insisted that someone summon him so that he could sit in as a visitor. As he entered, we noticed that he came prepared with a memo pad and pen in hand. We assumed that he intended to grade his manager, with intent to share his findings at a later date. Although he was invited to observe, he intentionally dominated the meeting, to our manager's disbelief, not affording her the opportunity to discuss anything within the two hour timeframe. He polled the room individually and collectively, asking each of us *"if we had the necessary tools that we needed in order to perform our jobs effectively?"*

When it was my time to speak, I asked for a company cell phone and pager as he wrote down each of our requests beside our names, respectively. Quite naturally, we didn't see anything wrong until which time he polled the room again asking for clarification to our requests. Unlike the others, I never waivered from my initial request. Honestly, I didn't believe that I'd receive these things but what was wrong with asking? The Bible says *"we get not because we ask not."* Surely that statement does not apply to me.

As she sat for hours fuming during this debacle, the aura that she was giving off alerted me to the fact that she had grown weary with the groups' antics. He rendered her absolutely speechless! I'd prepared myself for the tsunami that was about to overtake the entire group as soon as her boss exited, whistling as usual. Some employees considered the whistling to be sarcastic and condescending. Not me. That's what set him apart from others. In other words, that was his trademark. I welcome individuality within the scope of reason. But, everything has its place.

Once he closed the door, her eyes swirled around to everyone in attendance and I immediately felt a cold draft! We thought we'd become extras in an Exorcist sequel as she lit into us! Her angry exact words were, *"I do not believe you people, you all believe whatever he says, you don't believe any of what I say! How dare you!"* How dare she say such a thing to her employees! Her anger was misdirected indeed. I've always wondered what *"you people"* mean? I hate it when anyone addresses an entire group as *"you people!"* That's a sign of disrespect. Other than asking about supplies, he hadn't discussed anything else with the group. So, can someone explain the source of her derogatory statements.

Instead of taking her frustration out on her employees, she should have been upset with her own boss! Immediately, two or three coworkers attempted to calm her down but the rant-raving continued. She leaped from her chair, cut their explanations short by throwing up her hands shouting, *"WHATEVER!"* as she proceeded to leave, slamming the door behind her. Should we take that to mean the meeting had concluded? To note, someone important within this organization once exclaimed, *"Just because a person has the credentials required for a managerial position, once given the opportunity does not necessarily guarantee that this same individual will be successful in management."* This comment applies to several managers I know, but I'm left scratching my head in amazement. Why was this sentiment expressed to the IRS community via e-mail? It would have been interesting to know exactly which manager(s) he had in mind.

With the exception of yours truly, everyone else in the conference room was dumbfounded with their mouths hanging open. Shameless to say, I was filing my nails while all of this nonsense was taking place. I was not surprised because I'd experienced her *"attitude"* beforehand. What people fail to realize is that this is a business. One's personal feelings should take a back seat in any organization, especially one as large as the IRS. Unfortunately, some managers are not able to differentiate between business and personal!

As a form of payback, as well as to further exacerbate matters, she approached and accused several of us of not meeting our deadlines in responding to taxpayer requests for refund(s). In her hand, she held a monthly report that outlined the number of refunds that needed to be issued, according to the assigned employee number. Because we knew that to be incorrect, a coworker and I printed the report respectively from our computers. As we approached the manager to discuss the findings of her report versus our own, she said *"why is it always the two of you?!"* We looked at one another in amazement to her nasty question.

As she entered her office, we followed close behind. While she was speaking with my peer, I noticed another report on her desk that displayed my name in highlights. Quite naturally I asked, *"what report is this?"* She hollered at me saying, *"Alita, if you'll be patient, I'll get to you in a minute!"* I looked sideways at her before excusing myself from her office. Sometime thereafter, I was advised that the manager was going to apologize later for her earlier bout of unprofessionalism. Although I worked very hard to make this manager look good, she openly expressed to others whom she considered to be her best employee.

I wasn't in the running, as if my work was slouchy. The employee whom she placed on a pedestal is the one whom others feel submits mediocre work, leaving a lot to be desired. When you're comfortable with yourself and your own abilities, you don't have to compete with others. I didn't feel the need to have to. Later that evening my manager cornered me in the bathroom as I braced myself, unsure of what was about to transpire. To my surprise, she asked that I forgive her regarding her tone earlier. Her one request was that we *"pinky swear"* as a sign of reconciliation. Pinky swear? Are you kidding? I have not taken this oath since childhood. Far be it from that, I accepted her apology.

Anyway, my sincerity should not have been questioned. Hers on the other hand was debatable. Sometime thereafter, this female manager secretly reported me to TIGTA, but I was unaware of that one fact until months later. How deceptive of her, smiling in my face and stabbing me with a *"jagged edged"* sword! That's why it's hard for some people to trust others. Once lost, TRUST is the one thing that's hard to recoup, no matter the mitigating circumstances involved. What a deceptive attempt at false redemption, coming from a so-called Christian.

SEGMENT TWO

THE CALM
BEFORE THE STORM

CHAPTER VII

One morning the entire department was summoned together for an impromptu standup meeting to announce that the Chief (SPB) would be leaving the IRS. The day of the announcement would be his last day. We were not told why he was leaving the Service, only that he'd be leaving for much bigger and better things. (As I stated earlier, when a manager leaves, their future seems to be brighter but when a lower level employee leaves, it's via termination. Talk about double standards). Shock was the one emotion all of us displayed. Immediately, I knew that I would miss him. I still do.

Before he departed, he asked *"Alita, where do you see yourself in five years? I do not want to return later to find that you're still a Technician."* His expectations of me were high, obviously he had the utmost belief in my capabilities to excel within the organization. I joked with him and said, *"who knows, five years from now I might be the District Director of IRS in Houston."* Because of his love of music, he often referred to me as the legendary Josephine Baker, commenting that I reminded him of her. He smiled, we shook hands and he was gone that Friday evening. Despite what's been said or implied, some people have a way of leaving imprints upon your heart. He will always be remembered for doing just that. Godspeed, my friend.

The following Monday morning, we were introduced to the new Chief of the department, the first African American male to ever hold that position. (His arrival was planned because there is no way someone could have reported to the office in that capacity on such short notice). Prior to his appointment, personnel announced *"TEMPORARY"* GS 1101-9 Bankruptcy Specialist positions, not to exceed (NTE) one year. Naturally, I applied for the position along with a few of my coworkers.

Weeks later, I was considered to be a best qualified candidate via Personnel. Interviews were held, I was promoted, whereas I served in this temporary position for fifty weeks. Two weeks shy of the year, this position was announced as permanent and anyone who sought consideration needed to apply.

Management intentionally announced this position prior to my having reached one year, otherwise protocol would be to promote without further competition. It goes without saying that protocol wasn't followed. Although I was two (2) weeks shy of the required one year, management DEMOTED me back to a GS 7 Technician. In 2000, I applied for this permanent position, was promoted and transferred from group to group, this time to work for a Caucasian female.

Initially, when I was promoted in June 99 to the temporary position, the specialized experience that I had acquired as a Technician was sufficient for advancement to Specialist. When the vacancy announcement was posted for permanent placement, the requirements were that all other internal/external applicants possess a Bachelor's, Master's or Ph.D. to be eligible for consideration. Upon reviewing the document, I commented to a few coworkers, *"since when is it a requirement for a Bankruptcy Specialist to have all of these qualifications to be considered for a promotion? I further said, "Goodness, if I had all of these skills I would be employed elsewhere."* The comment was not made to take a jab at my employer. The thing that I found to be most peculiar is that these same qualifications were not required a year prior to, nor were they required of others in the Service.

After I allowed my thought processes to kick in, I realized that the vacancy announcement was worded as such in attempts to persuade outside employees from applying. Because several interested candidates already were performing Specialist duties, we automatically had the necessary credentials for consideration, based on the level of specialized experience attained over the years, which was a substitute for the educational requirements. The Agency maliciously exercised its weed out policy—they were well aware that employees in other areas of government would be deemed ineligible. How dastardly! In other words, their intent was for nine employees only to apply/reapply so that we'd be promoted.

In attempts to diffuse the conversation that we were engaged in, this chief hurriedly approached from out of nowhere asking, *"Don't you ladies have work to do?"* As I proceeded to my work area, I jokingly asked *"what happened to freedom of speech?"* That was a mistake! At a moment's notice, he became belligerent, yelling and hollering at me asking *"Alita, are you being insubordinate?!"* My response was no, but he continued to yell and scream in my work area, in my ear and in the presence of coworkers seated close by. Then he said, *"I need to see you and your manager in my office ASAP!"* When I told him that my manager was out of the office, he exclaimed that he needed to see both of us first thing the next morning, he was going to *"put me in my place once and for all!"* His words verbatim. Why did he follow me to my work area? Why was he so angry? Seems as though he was expecting an ugly verbal exchange.

Obviously, he was pissed off with the *"freedom of speech"* comment or maybe someone had irritated him very early that morning, taking his frustrations out on me. Honestly, I had no idea that he would become so unraveled because we kidded with one another often. This time it backfired on me. If I am not mistaken, he has a military background whereas he holds a high ranking position, probably Colonel. Ooh wee, that's why I never enlisted! A witness to this incident stated that this male chief was so close upon me that the hairs on my neck should have raised! Although his actions were inflammatory, I was able to maintain my composure only because I remained silent and kept my back turned. Otherwise, the outcome would have been totally different! Honestly, remaining silent was an absolute hard thing to do! No one likes to be yelled at, especially in the workplace in the presence of others. Imagine the outcome had the scripts been flipped.

Because my manager was out of the office the day before, I documented what transpired so as to discuss the matter with her upon her arrival to work, hurriedly seeking union representation because this appeared to be serious. A union official whom I was very familiar with, agreed to attend the meeting with me but had a prior engagement, advising me not to attend without her. Hours later, my manager approached my workstation and said, *"we're ready for you."* I mentioned that my union representative was not available. She said, *"We have someone for you."*

At that moment it was clear to me that a conspiracy had formed. Based on her demeanor, management had discussed and hatched their devious plot prior to summoning me. Otherwise, the meeting would have been conducted first thing that morning instead of hours later. But oh no, management needed time to strategize! Why was my own manager upset with me?

Since I had no say in this matter, I thought to myself you're being set up! Because I did not want to give the impression of being insubordinate, I signed off the computer and proceeded to the chief's office with my manager close behind on my heels, leading me to the slaughterhouse. With each step, the noose around my neck tightened as I proceeded to the death chamber! Instinctively, I felt trouble brewing because my manager was walking too fast! Due to her double plus measurements, I had no earthly idea she could move so swiftly. Never judge a book by its cover, looks can be deceiving.

Luckily, a male union representative was present, someone who I had no knowledge of nor had I ever seen before that day. He introduced himself and asked permission to represent me. The meeting began as the male management official explained the reason(s) we were there. From its inception, he spoke an untruth! He stated that he had given me a directive that I did not follow, therefore I was insubordinate. Instinctively, I attempted to interject in defense of myself by advising him that he had accused me unjustly.

As soon as I asked for my witnesses to appear, he cut me off by saying, *"Alita this is not a trial!"* Although he was correct about that one thing, he acted as if he was judge, jury and executioner. Things were so intense, for a moment he actually looked and sounded like a prosecutorial attorney. Better yet, this management official could have been an exceptional cast member in any legal drama on the big screen, as it relates to debates. With one exception, he did not afford me the opportunity to debate.

Having said that, to speak during that conference period was forbidden and off limits, until which time he gave the go ahead to do so! To reiterate, a conversation does not exist between two people when one person dominates the platform. He talked and rant raved so long, I forgot exactly what I had intended to say. Whatever I'd intended to say didn't matter anymore. Maybe that was his intent. Almost instantaneously, I became frustrated and crestfallen at his attempts to silence me. It felt as if his feet were pressed against my throat to stifle all breathing processes.

As his voice commanded everyone's attention, I got the distinct impression he does not like losing arguments. He must have the absolute last word or else! Days later, I still heard his belligerent words while I slept. Sometimes it's good to let a person think they're *"large and in charge"*, especially men. When I'm wrong, I'm the first to admit it via an apology. However, this man wasn't going to concede, especially not to a woman and not to a subordinate. Nevertheless, I remained silent by respecting his status, aside from the fact that he disrespected me and everyone else in the workgroup.

During the entire encounter, my group manager sat there and watched as he belittled me, saying and doing absolutely nothing in my defense. Based on her demeanor, it was almost as if she was savoring the moment. Because she was out of the office the day before, you'd think she'd question me about the prior incident, or at least have some input as my first-line manager. Oh no, she didn't utter a mumbling word, maintaining a hypnotic stance as if she was programmed!

The union steward asked, *"Was Alita insubordinate?"* He said *"No, she was not insubordinate, I don't like her attitude!"* Sound familiar? Why is it that an employee is charged with having an attitude when they attempt to defend themselves against management? I don't understand. On the other hand, yes I do. If you go against the grain, you've overstepped your boundary. What's ok for management is not acceptable for the employee. Double standard?

My manager was instructed to write me up, referencing the Rules of Conduct, stressing that if anything of this nature happens in the future, I will be subject to disciplinary actions. Now I'm really confused. If I hadn't done anything wrong according to this managerial official, why was I threatened with a written admonishment?

Again I state, any time an employee attempts to stand against management's wrongdoing, they incur long drawn out death sentences, with the terms of their punishment to be served in months to years of sheer agony! Notably so, I was still bewildered, wondering what had I done to warrant such extreme measures. Better yet, who was going to reprimand him for his conduct unbecoming?!

*** *"The true measure of a man is not where he stands in moments of comfort and convenience. Ultimately, what matters most is how firmly planted his feet are during challenging and controversial times."* ***

CHAPTER VIII

Clearly, there was absolutely no reason for this manager to become so enraged about my comment alone. I presume that maybe he was having a bad day and I just happened to be in the line of fire. It's a fact that we all have bad days, what's important is how we tend to deal with them. Unbeknownst to anyone, I forgave him and we never spoke about the incident afterwards. Perhaps, there was an underlying issue that wasn't evident earlier on. As time passed, I realized that he was following a directive from his superiors.

Management was angry with me and a few of my peers because we filed grievances against the Agency, alleging unlawful employment practices, prohibited personnel practices and denial of upward mobility, etc. During conversation with this management official, he would comment for us grievants to *"forget about the past, let it go, move on."* Some things are easier said than done. After a person has been misused and abused so often, quite naturally they become embittered, especially if they're being trampled on by the same culprits. Not everyone is willing to kiss and makeup as if nothing ever transpired. Nevertheless, I don't spite those who forgive/forget without a second thought.

If you ask me, his sentiment is equivalent to saying that our yesterdays are insignificant. To whom it may concern, I will NEVER forget. It's in our remembering that we have been molded and shaped into whatever we've become, good or bad. Yet, I wonder if he has forgotten about his past and the *"comments"* directed at him, along with the many wrongs that he encountered and was expected to endure as he attempted to climb the corporate ladder. I can guarantee that his rise to success didn't take off without a hitch! Literally, *"If we resign ourselves to forget about our past, our futures are doomed."* Other than our names and identities, the past is the only thing that we own because it has attached itself to us like Siamese twins.

With all due respect, the past should be the venue that leads to reparations but it takes some effort, nevertheless. Yes, we've waited long enough for our forty acres and a mule! It's been so long, our forty acres have been reduced to twenty and the mule has become something unrecognizable. I distinctly recall how he felt years ago when he was passed over for a promotion, whereas several other non-qualified Caucasian males were promoted over him. He closed himself off to the world and we all knew what he was experiencing, even without him having advised us of the dilemma. Far be it from that, he was elevated the next *"go around"* as if that's ok. Why is it that *"we"* as a people always have to wait? That's a question for the masses to answer, although I, along with many others know the real reason.

HISTORY-----In June 1998, NTEU filed a Mass Grievance under the procedures of its Collective Bargaining Agreement, on behalf of the Plaintiffs and seven other minority employees against the Agency. The grievance alleged that the IRS owed Plaintiff's back pay for approximately five (5) years. Sometime in November 1998, NTEU invoked arbitration in this matter.

There were repeated attempts made to contact the Union field office regarding an expected arbitration date, without success. Therefore, on April 14, 2000, the Plaintiff's filed an informal EEO complaint against IRS management and NTEU officials, alleging Discrimination and Retaliation based on their actions in the mass grievance process. Five months later, Plaintiff's filed a formal EEO complaint alleging the same issues that were raised in the initial complaint. However, Plaintiff's did not prevail in this arena. So, Plaintiff's then filed a civil action in federal court in the United States District Court (Southern District of Texas-Houston Division) on August 30, 2001. As a matter of fact, the civil suit was dismissed on July 2, 2002.

Because of my tenacious and outspoken nature, management has always accused me of spearheading complaints because I was second in command as Class Agent. For these reasons and more, I was retaliated and reprised against in its ugliest form.

Since that time, management's assertion is that I have the ability to sway people. Aha, the truth surfaces. *"If there is no nucleus, there is no center."*

Although I wholeheartedly disagree with their assertion, I'll only admit to being the glue that held everything together. However, you already know what happens when glue no longer bonds. Yep, things fall apart. It's common knowledge that this male chief was personally asked by the former District Director to relocate to Houston from Colorado, in attempts to *"SQUASH"* our issues. That was his number one priority.

One day in particular, the District Director had the audacity to gather together a collective group of minority females within the department to discuss the *"GLASS CEILING"* of all things. He stated that he *"understood our plight because being a Hispanic male (minority) in the "establishment", he has experienced some of the same injustices we had, such as being passed over for promotions, etc. when in fact he knew that he was more qualified and deserving of the position versus his Caucasian counterparts."*

As he spoke, I was without emotion, pondering what to feel or think about his revelations. Despite this, someone exclaimed, *"Aw, he feels our pain."* For the record, if he felt our pain, we wouldn't still be in pain after all of these years! First, if he really cared about our pain, the issues could have been resolved as easily as snapping his fingers. He was the authority figure. Second, if you willingly admit that the system is broken, fix it!

Once the Agency realized exactly what it would take to resolve the matter financially, we all became expendable! Unknowingly so and to the grievants' surprise later on, the Agency and NTEU proffered a settlement agreement that brought about the creation of fourteen positions within our department, positions that we had to compete for in order to receive consideration. Where or what was the benefit in all of this for us? These entities' actions constitute COLLUSION!

CHAPTER IX

Ironically, months later I was summoned to testify in an EEO hearing against this same male managerial official, regarding a Sex Discrimination complaint (I believe) that had been filed by one of his female managers. Just to let you know what was thought of me, I wasn't notified until two days before the hearing via e-mail with instructions on where/when to report. Insightfully so, I wasn't even worthy of notification via phone call.

Oh, now the Agency is soliciting aid from me in attempts to solidify a victory. On the flip side, the opposing team expected me to say anything defamatory and inflammatory against him in this process to help seal his fate. Ain't that a blip! Do I look like *"Sally Sausage Head?"*

As I stepped off the elevator proceeding to the waiting room, I was greeted by a posse of managers who smiled and verbalized hellos, although many of them had never spoken a word to me prior to that day. Yes, I was familiar with each of them by name (and history) but had never worked for either of them directly, with the exception of one male Caucasian individual who sat close by. Their reaction to me was quite peculiar. It was almost as if they liked me, but I was born at night not last night! They needed me.

What was obvious early on is that I had just stepped into the lion's den. They pounced on me quick, fast and in a hurry, as if I was a piece of bloody meat! If allowed, someone would have pulled out a chair for me very close to them I'm sure. Even with that, there was an ulterior motive.

Each of them were current managers under my former chief's tutelage. Each were Caucasian, males and female. I, along with my former female manager was African American. I am in no way insinuating that my feelings were race based, the opposing party made it such. With that being said, I've always tried to be on the right side of any issue, regardless of one's race.

Nevertheless, it's a known fact that his managers did not approve of him because he held all of them to the same standards, according to policy.

Unbeknownst to many, someone in the office specifically referred to him as *"Napoleon Bonaparte"* after introductions when his back was turned. Coward! This individual further stated that the African American manager should *"go back to Africa where he came from! Further saying that "he is so short, I had to bend down to shake his hand."* These comments were overheard by others during private conversations held in the offices of his Caucasian and Hispanic counterparts, all the while they laughed incessantly. Having said that, this just goes to show how others feel and think about certain employees, regardless of their title or status in life. Obviously, he posed a threat to someone.

It's a sad state of affairs to have to report that although we live in the twenty first century, there are others within this society who still judge us by the *"color of our skin and not by the content of our character."* No matter how successful we become, we'll never be treated as equal, we'll always be treated like second-class citizens and looked upon as *"NIGGERS"* in the eyes of some. That's why it's imperative that we conduct ourselves accordingly by always doing the *"right thing."*

To date, we've only taken *baby steps"* toward the finish line and we're only going to be allowed to advance within the organization when the ok is rendered, not a minute beforehand. However, as for his expectations as Territory Manager, there were no exceptions, no special privileges for anyone. That was an absolute hard pill for his managers to swallow!

Within days, the object of the game changed drastically. These managers were not willing to accept change because they had become too familiar with the norm. Or is it safe to say that they had a problem accepting authority from an African American manager who has attained executive level status? Excuse my French, but that *"good ole boy"* network that was customary in the organization prior to this individual's appointment ceased almost immediately. These same managers scurried like terrified squirrels to find jobs elsewhere far away from him. Isn't it funny how the tables turn so quickly?

Where is the Agency when employees cry out for help? Some of us have been disavowed and treated as if our complaints have no credence (when in fact you know otherwise) and made to feel that we are indeed unimportant human beings, let alone employees. The moment arrived and I was expected to play that *"so-called game"* my manager speaks of so liberally. To everyone's dismay, I asked for clarification each time a question was posed to me regarding his character. That's well within my right to do if I'm unsure about exactly what's being asked of me. I'd hate to commit perjury wouldn't I? Just because he and I had had an unpleasant altercation months earlier, that does not give anyone the right to capitalize on our misfortune.

If the attorneys could have gotten away with it, I would have been tossed out of that room on my head! Because I had nothing to contribute for either side, once it was evident that my testimony wasn't going to be useful, I was angrily advised by the Administrative Judge that *"my services were not needed"*, even before my chair warmed!   If I am not mistaken, she was angry with me for not participating and contributing to this process. If her position is a neutral one, why was she angry? Hence, I bypassed being a *"stool pigeon"* in this nonsense by refusing to play their little game after being badgered during questioning. CHECKMATE! However, the games continue. Darn it, the world could have been my oyster if I'd played along. As it stands, I've never liked oysters! Now I know why.

For the record, this judge has presided over several discrimination complaints (filed by employees), whereas her involvement should be neutral and non-biased. Now I find myself asking this question: "Was the correct decisions rendered in each and every case based on the facts presented? Or was the edge given to the Agency attorneys because of their advanced knowledge of case law?" Hmm.........

To compound matters, moments before I was called to appear upstairs to render testimony, my acting manager (male) pulled up a chair alongside me and asked pointblank, *"Alita what are you going to testify to?"(* This manager is friends with the former male chief whom I'd had the altercation with earlier). Sensing that he knew what I was thinking based on how I looked at him, he immediately tried to clean up the question, stating *"I'm here*

to warn you to be careful—the hearing is going to be recorded."
This is a policy violation as it relates to the EEO process,
commonly referred to as interference.

Common sense dictates that if my manager felt that my
testimony would be useless, there would have been no need to
"warn" me. But because of my prior, unsavory altercation with
his boss months earlier, management was unsure what I'd testify
to, if anything at all. Since I had been referred to as a loose
cannon, they pulled out all stops to frighten me into backing off.
Management had a lot to lose they felt. However, their bullying
did not frighten me one iota. In spite of this, my manager insisted
on sparring with me as I disregarded his attempt at self-
gratification. Often times, it felt as if I walked around with a
bull's-eye on my forehead. Enough can't be said about the
games people play. Immediately, I informed him that he was
interfering and meddling in the EEO process, which is a policy
violation. That was my first mistake!

Furthermore, I informed him that I do not need to be coached
in this process. I'm not prepared to step out on a limb and say
that my manager's boss encouraged him to provoke an
altercation with me regarding my testimony, then again I'm not
prepared to rule it out either. This intimidation tactic was
practiced daily to advise me *"if I slipped up and said the wrong
thing, I would regret it later."* Although I ignored my manager's
threats, he grew more agitated with me because I knew and
exercised my protected rights against him and the Agency. When
I mentioned to him that he was out of line in approaching me
about my testimony, he grew extremely furious, looking
possessed! This was my absolute second mistake! Read on.

Instantly, I thought I saw a pitchfork in his hand and horns
sprout on the top of his head when he jumped from his chair,
mumbling something under his breath as he turned to leave! He
would become so angry with me, he'd often talk to himself.
Days later, I received negative documentation leading up to the
ending of my rating period. This was my manager's way of
alerting me to the fact that he was in control. Because of
managements' retaliatory antics, this didn't come as a surprise to
me. For the record, if management insists on being anti-
employee, they shouldn't be so transparent.

Days later, in an attempt to catch me in a vulnerable state, he summoned me to his office to discuss what transpired during the hearing, once again. Didn't I mention earlier that he was meddling and interfering in the EEO process? When I did not reveal anything concrete to him, he angrily demanded that I leave his office! What's wrong with this picture? If I'd been an eager beaver with any gossip to report, he would not have allowed me to leave his office. My mother is a firm believer that real men don't gossip. I'm inclined to agree.

As I was getting up from the chair, attempting to straighten it back to its original position, my manager charged at me full force, almost catching me with my back turned. Again I state, coward! When he finally caught himself and applied the brakes, we were almost nose to nose. In self-defense, I threw up my hands asking, *"what are you going to do, are you going to hit me?! His response was "if I hit you, you won't get up!"* I was not shocked one bit at this admission. Had he hit me, quite naturally I would have hit him back because that's what human nature dictates. Third strike, CONDEMNATION!

If I know him like I think I know him, he would have spoken another untruth, accusing me of hitting him, although I would have had the bruise in my face to substantiate that an assault occurred. Based on management's past actions, I would have been dismissed and he would still be sitting in an office somewhere wreaking havoc after committing so many documented injustices against his employees. It stands to reason, that if my manager thought he could get away with hitting me, he would have done just that! Remember, I am speaking about an employee who was only an acting management official at the time of this occurrence. If his actions were brazen then, can you imagine how quickly things spun out of control when he was elevated to a permanent manager in Insolvency?! Yes, I said permanent.

And, these sorts of comments are spoken on a daily basis and reported to EEO with no adverse repercussions forthcoming for management. The following pages will explain the AGONY that I endured for many, many years because I protected myself against management by lodging complaints of retaliation, reprisal and discrimination via EEO/NTEU. If you stop reading at this point, you will truly regret it. Why? Because the very best is yet to come! *"Commit thy way into the Lord, trust also in him, and he shall bring it to pass. And he shall bring forth thy righteousness as the light, and thy judgment as the noonday. Rest in the Lord, and wait patiently for him; fret not because of him who prospered in his way; because of the man who bringeth wicked devices to pass. Cease from anger and forsake wrath; fret not thyself in any wise to do evil. For evildoers shall be cut off; but those that wait upon the Lord, they shall inherit the earth."*

Psalms 37: 5-9

CHAPTER X

In September 2001, weeks after the 911 tragedy, my female manager left the department, accepting a position at the satellite office. To no one's surprise, she cleared her office while we employees attended a training session in Dallas, deciding to celebrate her birthday privately. She didn't even stick around long enough for the ink to dry on her paperwork! We knew that she was leaving but we were unaware of her departure date. However, lots of controversy brewed in the office days later because three of her employees were secretly reported to TIGTA for investigation.

Needless to say, I was one of three employees subjected to scrutiny. Two of us had filed union grievances against her months earlier, and the other employee was one whom she absolutely despised. Because the investigations yielded nothing conclusive, all three of the cases were closed NO ACTION. How ironic?

We were not aware that we had been under investigation, until which time the acting male manager called us into the office individually and collectively to advise us of such! Again, we were unsuspecting. Without a doubt, this was her way of getting back at us for filing grievances against her. I guess this was her last chance to dominate and exert control over her employees before leaving the department. You big baby! In October 2001, the acting male manager was appointed to replace her, until which time a permanent manager was chosen. Prior to her departure, she advised me that her replacement just might be worse than her. As she mentioned this, I thought to myself, *"I don't think so."* It didn't take long for me to realize exactly how correct she was! His management style is unethical, unprofessional and the absolute worst of any manager whom I had ever worked for! *"You know what you got, but you don't know what you're going to get."*

One day when I was retrieving mail from my mailbox, I noticed that a claim objection had been placed there for me to resolve. A **claim objection** is a legal document that's filed by a debtor's attorney opposing the IRS's proof of claim. A **proof of claim** is the primary method creditors have of receiving payment, as it relates to the bankruptcy proceedings. It lists the debtor's liability to creditors, respectively. Once I queried the case number, I immediately placed the document in another employees' mailbox. For the simple reason, the debtor's exorbitant tax liability exceeded the GS-1101/9 and the GS 1101/11 dollar criteria. Therefore, sole responsibility belonged to the GS 12 Revenue Officer/Advisor.

Hours later, that same document resurfaced in my mailbox. That's when I sought assistance from my manager regarding this delicate matter. Once we discussed the issue, my manager agreed that the responsibility lied elsewhere and he in turn reassigned the debtor's case/objection to the higher graded employee. This male individual cursed out the manager and advised him that *"he was not going to respond to that objection!"* Guess what? He did not. So, the correspondence was rerouted to my mailbox for resolution. Ok, here we go again playing musical chairs.

Once I realized what was happening, I responded to the legal document immediately. In the best interest of the customer, this was a necessity. As it stands, there is a ten day turnaround for a response to be forwarded to the IRS's legal department. If no response to this document is received, the IRS stands a good chance of losing thousands of dollars because the government's interest wasn't protected. At the very least, the debtor's case floats around in a suspended status, holding up confirmation until which time all issues are resolved surrounding the need to having have filed the objection in the first place.

Why penalize the taxpayer by failing to respond in a timely fashion? Before the close of business that day, I attempted once more to appeal to my manager's sense of judgment, to no avail. He refused to listen to anything I had to say, work related. However, before I turned to leave, he handed me a document that required my signature. I'd been written up. Imagine that.......

Just as you figured, that's when my problems began with my manager, when in April 2002, he stated *"you'll be hurting yourself for FUTURE promotional opportunities as they arise by refusing to respond to claim objections!"* Did he know something that I didn't? By stating this, he makes it seem as though I failed to follow a directive, which is entirely false.

I only attempted to remind my manager that it was incumbent upon the GS 12 Revenue Officer/Advisor to resolve the issue based on its complexity and the dollar criteria associated with the objection, according to the Case Assignment Guide (CAG). Because my manager was furious but afraid to reprimand him, he took out his frustration on me through reassignment. Out of anger, my manager threatened ME and wrote ME up for speaking out about protocol, whereas this male employee received no verbal or written reprimand.

I have legitimate reason(s) to believe that my fate had been discussed by my first-line manager as well as to other levels of management across the territory, relating to the competitive selection process. Otherwise, my manager would not have been so adamant, speaking with certainty about future promotional opportunities. All along, management had an ulterior motive. How deceptive! In attempts to further punish me, I became my manager's personal whipping dog because I did not stay *"in my place like a good little girl!"* Four months later in August 2002, I was denied the opportunity to compete and interview for a promotional position in this department, when I had been identified as a best qualified candidate via Personnel.

As a further form of punishment, I was once again denied this same opportunity in September 2002, when one other best-qualified candidate was interviewed. Weeks later, this individual was the selectee for the promotion in Houston, whereas the candidate in Austin who placed first on the selection certificate was promoted three months later, from the same certificate and allowed to remain in the Austin office, despite the fact that the vacancy announcement listed Houston as the ONLY post-of-duty. As a matter of fact, the Agency asserts that there was only one vacancy. You decide......

Sometime after my manager received permanent placement, he summoned two of my peers and me to an impromptu meeting in the conference room, supposedly to discuss inventory assignments. As he began to speak, we looked at one another in awe because the concept that he explained was contrary to policy. When we attempted to interject by asking questions, he started jumping around in his chair, hollering at us stating *"Ok Ms. Carter, how would you handle it?"* Now he was really irritated! My response was, *"if you have a team of four, in order for the inventories to be balanced, I would split all twenty six alphabets accordingly to achieve manageability."* Obviously my manager did not like my concept.

He looked up, threw his hands around very swiftly, pointing his fingers in my face shouting, *"SHUT UP, SHUT UP, what you're stating is ASININE!"* He almost stuck me in the eye! What gives this manager the right to think that his ludicrous conduct is acceptable? To everyone's dismay, his misconduct has been accepted by Agency management for years! And, he's still a manager to date.

CHAPTER XI

My manager's actions were totally unprofessional and unwarranted. On the other hand, had one of us acted in the manner in which he performed, we would have been reprimanded and probably suspended (or worse) for causing dissension. You see, that's where the term double standard is coined. Management's philosophy is *"Do as I say, not as I do."* It's acceptable for them to act this way, employees better not or else! What's so insidious about all of this is that he has the uncanny ability to come off as if he's the victim. If it's true that adjectives describe, the word that fits him best is VINDICTIVE. Obviously his superiors are accepting and approving of his behavior, it's still ongoing.

I can see two reasons why this type of behavior is being allowed. First, maybe upper management doesn't care about the employees. Second, maybe they are letting him tighten the rope around his own neck, whereas in the end he'll be the scapegoat. When the dust settles, his superiors will have departed from the organization via retirement, traveling around the world, enjoying themselves. He will not be afforded that luxury because he'll be stuck here answering questions, such as *"What role did you play?"* It's funny how he has pledged total allegiance to his employer. With much assurance, I guarantee that the feelings will not be reciprocal in the end when it matters most.

In the interim, there will be no deals made, no mitigating factors to consider. Therefore, his status as manager along with his retirement will be in jeopardy. If justice prevails, at that moment I'm sure he'll fully understand the true meaning of inequity. Now is the time to exclaim, *"Aw, he feel our pain"* because he will have walked that mile in all of our shoes! Someone should pass that brother a mirror! Obviously, he has forgotten about the struggle. Having said that, NO EMPLOYEE should be allowed to exercise dominance over others because of their status within any organization.

Accountability should be the focus. When has that policy ever taken hold where management is concerned? Mindful to say, accountability is the focus when subordinates commit wrongs. Throughout the entire time that he was performing, one of my peers sat silently as our manager criticized me and another peer. That's when I asked to be excused from this witch hunt, not wanting to allow his vicious campaign of ridicule to continue. Truth be told, that was my lunch break.

With much reluctance he relented and I excused myself from the room. However, my peers stayed on in attempts to clear things up with him. About ten minutes later, I noticed that one of them had returned to their respective work station because the climate had become extremely hostile in the conference room! Our manager was upset once again. As expected, we reported the incident to NTEU and EEO.

As expected, both of our evaluative appraisals were lowered without adequate documentation, absent any written negative reviews that warranted its lowering. This is commonly referred to as REPRISAL. As a result, the employee who remained "silent" throughout was rewarded days later. In other words, she received an exorbitant monetary award based on the fact that her numerical rating increased significantly, although this individual's work performance left a lot to be desired.

This is a prime example of how some employees in the department are treated differently from others, depending on how management feels about them. If you're quiet and don't cause interruptions to management's methodically flawed plans, you'll reap the benefits and any/all other incentives that's offered, including promotions, even if you're not deserving of such. On the other hand, if you go against the grain BEWARE!! These actions are disparate, which creates a discriminatory impact on employees who are similarly situated. Days later, my manager stood in the work area conversing with others, advising several of my peers that *"Alita Carter and her cohort have issues, further stating that we are hard to get along with and that he does not like to entertain certain employee comments because of our argumentative nature."* HOUSTON, we have a problem!

What's awful is that this same manager allowed my cohort's peers to enter his office frequently with complaints about her work, complaining that she did not know her job, she made too many mistakes in completing her work assignments and that she was too old to perform her job duties satisfactorily. This individual would print the entity screen of taxpayer cases, identify the mistakes made using red ink and forward the documents to our manager as evidence to use against her for evaluative purposes. That was his "crème de la crème." He absolutely loved the bickering that existed between certain employees in the office, bickering that he contributed to and should take credit for its many occurrences!

Instead of advising the troublemaker that he did not need her assistance, as far as reviews are concerned, he capitalized on the opportunity to make someone's life a living hell! What's ludicrous is that the employee who brought these things to his attention was not his employee. Then again, he salivated and absolutely enjoyed moments like this because it provided an avenue for him to discuss terrible things amongst the peer group, because of a strong dislike between the two employees. This practice absolutely should not be tolerated. It causes division amongst employees, creating dissension that poisons the work environment as a whole.

When the manager was questioned about his actions and comments made during the meeting he stated, *"I would never say anything like that to an employee."* Liar, liar pants on fire! In order to convince himself that he had not stated these things, he approached the work group again, threatening some and demanding that they admit he was being falsely accused. For the record, the workgroup was not present during that debacle.

Therefore, any attempt to rush to judgment in defense of him is useless. How can there be four people in a room but only one person's interpretation differs from the others in attendance? *"It amazes me to constantly witness employees going along to get along, by selling their souls to the Devil. I have been known to break tradition a time or two. However, that's why I can boldly look in the mirror and not DETEST my own reflection as it stares back at me. In other words, I'll still love myself in the morning, with no regrets whatsoever."*

I have found that the lower on the totem pole you are, the less respect you receive from management with greater expectations and demands. To simplify things for you, the higher graded you are, LESS is expected and you're allowed to do less in terms of productivity. This practice is discriminatory but rampant in Insolvency and perhaps in other offices within the IRS. If you ask me, the concept is backwards. The higher up the scale you go, MORE should be expected, without qualms. At that point, you're looked upon as a leader with *"supposed"* expertise, whereas everyone should carry their own load!

Why should some be allowed to *"vacation"* on the job while others are constantly whipped with the straps of oppression?! Furthermore, why am I assigned two hundred plus cases as a GS 1101-9 when other higher-graded, similarly situated counterparts are sitting comfortably on less than fifty cases, regardless to what the case assignment guide dictates?!

In my department, certain employees are rewarded with reduced inventories almost quarterly, after having reached a certain plateau of seniority within the organization. Well, maybe the inventories are reduced because of proven inabilities of some to manage their responsibilities effectively! The majority of the workload is dumped on the lower graded employees, with managerial demands to resolve the cases, no matter the complexity. For instance, if

I advise my manager that large dollar cases should be reassigned to a higher graded GS 11/12 employee, he would not reassign the case. Better yet, he'd angrily demand that I work it through to resolution. Second, if I posed too many questions about having to resolve these high dollar cases, my manager would express his negative sentiments in writing when he'd share my midyear review, in attempts to lower my numerical rating(s) because I challenged him. I was questioning protocol due to his customary, discriminant actions.

What's so unfair is that if a higher graded employee was in receipt of inventory that they felt should be reassigned or perhaps informed the manager that they were bombarded with inventory and could not meet their deadlines, the manager would reassign the cases to lower graded employees, no questions asked. What about my impending deadlines? This manager did not care. Then again, it goes back to what I mentioned earlier about RESPECT. In order for the process to work, each individual employee must be valued. In saying so, VALUE and WORTH should not be determined by one's grade level!

According to the Case Assignment Guide (CAG), inventory should be assigned based on case complexity and dollar criteria. But then again, management operates on double standards by using and abusing this guide to fit into their hidden agenda when they deem it to be feasible, no matter what the policies, rules and regulations dictate. What baffles me is that senior executive level management has the audacity to express concerns about annual survey results, all the while they have firsthand knowledge of exactly what transpires behind these walls.

In April 2002, the Houston office was assigned a replacement Territory Manager from Phoenix. When he visited Houston for a Town Hall Meeting, I specifically asked a direct question. *"Do you review employee casework and Employee Personnel Files (EPF's) on your own or do you just initial off on documentation (evaluations) once it's received from management absent review?"* His response was *"no, if I did that I would not need a manager."* He sarcastically chuckled and said, *"I hope that'll do."* After all that some of us have endured here, he has the audacity to be arrogant! His response was old, callous and unsupportive of the employees' plight in Houston!

I would not have asked the question if there was no reasoning behind it. According to any Territory Manager's position description, he/she should review employee appraisals for error(s). If errors are found, the appraisal should be returned to their respective manager for corrections according to policy and not arbitrarily lowered because an employee exercised their rights through the EEO or NTEU process. How do I know this?

It's called research. If you are of the Caucasian persuasion or perhaps Hispanic, you will be promoted over an African American employee (matter of fact), regardless of your qualifications or lack thereof. Although this Territory Manager was reassigned to another locale in October 2007, the damage he caused lingers on. It is irreversible.

SEGMENT THREE

"IN PURSUIT OF
JUSTICE"

CHAPTER XII

Anytime promotional opportunities are announced within the territory, the selecting official is the Territory Manager. As you know, Personnel is responsible for ranking packages and sending the names of all best qualified candidates to management for consideration. If management chooses to forego the interview process, this individual can randomly select a candidate from the selection certificate. However, if management chooses to interview candidates for the announced vacancy, everyone who is similarly situated must be interviewed. This is a mandate, according to the Office of Personnel Management guidelines.

However, this Territory Manager stated that he considered several "other" factors in determining which candidates were worthy of appointments to promotional positions in Insolvency. This was not necessary because these same factors had been determined by Personnel once the names of the best qualified candidates were sent to him via the selection certificate. And, having to do this is not a part of his job requirement. In other words, he himself re-ranked the packages in attempts to weed out whatever candidate(s) he deemed unworthy! If you've participated in the complaints process, your chances were slim to none. Needless to say, I fell under that category. Again I state, not because of my lack of qualifications, it was due to the level of disdain that management had for me.

POLICY: According to Stage 4: The Selection Stage of the Civil Service Reform Act (CSRA) states: *"At this stage, management chooses an employee to fill the vacant position. The previous stages should have produced a list of candidates with basic qualifications who scored the highest in an evaluation of current performance and potential. The selecting official has a substantial amount of discretion in choosing from the list of the best qualified employees. He has the power to decide not to* *select anyone at all. We are concerned here with the action in which the official chooses someone to fill the vacant position. You will look here at the method of distinguishing among the best qualified candidates and the reasons for the choice itself. At this stage, you will be seeking a retroactive promotion with back pay and interest on the back pay."*

QUESTION: Was the selection proper?

ANSWER: A myth frequently repeated by management is: *"You can't grieve non-selection."*

This is not true if you prove improper consideration by the selecting official or you prove illegal discrimination which would warrant the filing of an unfair labor practice charge, a grievance, or an Equal Employment Opportunity Complaint.

"The selecting official does have a great deal of discretion in selecting from the best qualified list. However, ANY selection technique, such as interviewing the best qualifiedcandidates, MUST be uniformly applied. When this uniformity is breached, the grievant is entitled to relief." If you can show that the selection decision included such improper factors as race, sex, age, religion, politics, marital status, or union activity, you can win a retroactive promotion for the employee passed over. Furthermore, it states that *"Retroactive promotion remedies are normally found when an employee has been improperly denied a career ladder promotion or when there is a violation at the selection stage of a competitive promotion in the form of prohibited discrimination or anti-union animus."*

It stands to reason that POLICY was not adhered to in this matter as previously stated. See Attachment(s). Furthermore, when promotional opportunities are announced in Houston (and that's rare), the positions are never permanent, only temporary not to exceed one year, with the exception of a Hispanic female who was permanently promoted to a GS 1101-12 Bankruptcy Specialist position some time ago. Although she's a minority, she's not an African American! Nevertheless, in other offices within this territory, employees are promoted to permanent positions without any vacancies or vacancy announcements in existence.

In March 2002, I applied for a GS 1101-11 promotion within my department and was identified as a best qualified candidate via Personnel, along with four other candidates who were afforded the opportunity to compete and interview. I am the only Best/Highly qualified candidate omitted from the competitive selection process. Weeks later, a coworker entered my workstation and inquired about the upcoming interviews. I was puzzled and didn't know what she was speaking about. That's when she stated that our manager had just informed her when and where interviews would be held.

When I approached him to inquire about my interview, without hesitation he stated, *"Ms. Carter, you will not be interviewing for this position."* At the time that this statement was told to me, I was not aware that my name appeared on the selection certificate as best qualified. I did not become aware of this until which time this same coworker filed an EEO complaint based on her non-selection for the promotional position of GS 1101-11 Bankruptcy Specialist. When she received her investigative file at home, after careful review of its contents, she contacted me at home to advise me what she had discovered in that *"Pandora's Box."* Oddly enough, I was not ready to review the evidence that would so overwhelm me.

The very next day, I contacted a Human Resource Specialist in Laguna Niguel, Ca. for assistance. Upon speaking with a female employee, I identified myself and explained why I was calling. The Vacancy Announcement number of SBB-SBL-2513 was readily given as we spoke. Although I knew what the answer would be, I asked if *"I should have interviewed for this position also?"* Her response was, *"our office has been advised by IRS management that no one interviewed for that position."*

Now why would management inform Personnel of this if there wasn't anything illegal going on? Right then I knew that something had occurred that was questionable, at best. She conducted her own research as I waited. This was the longest five or ten minutes of my life. Naturally, it felt as if someone had pierced my heart with a dagger, causing me to bleed uncontrollably. Upon her return, she confirmed what I already knew to be true.

She concurred that my name was listed on the promotion certificate as Best Qualified, therefore I should have been afforded an interview. All that I knew to do was cry. No one deserves to have something of that nature happen to them. Even after discovering something so terrible, management still continues with their crusade to trample on you, mad because their devious plot was uncovered!

Let the record reflect, I am in no way insinuating that I would have walked away with the promotion. My assertion is that I deserved the same entitlement. There are absolutely no words that can express how I feel, even now years later. I firmly believe that one day, *"I'll regain the abundance that has been promised, by recouping what was taken from me. When that day comes, I'll rejoice ecstatically because I will have the victory."* Better yet, I declare that I am the victor.

CHAPTER XIII

In response to personnel's findings, I felt compelled to interject to correct her, by naming each best qualified candidate who interviewed in August 2002, as well as naming the candidate who interviewed a month later, in September 2002. If you're thinking what I'm thinking, you're absolutely correct. To have a candidate interview for the same position thirty days after the initial interview(s) are conducted, is adverse to policy and unlawful. I've heard of interviews flowing over to the next day but not thirty days!

Not only was this entire process unfair to me, it was also unfair to the candidates who interviewed earlier. The edge was given to the selectee, not them. and to reason, that if any of the candidates were unavailable to interview at the appointed time, protocol would have been to cancel the interviews all together and reschedule for a later date. This was not done.

Management continued with their deceptive plan of business as usual. Their intent all along was to deny me this opportunity but did not count on anyone finding out what actually transpired in this illegal process. Had they selected my comrade for the promotion, their scheme would still be a secret—because no other best qualified candidate would have grieved the matter, out of fear of reprisal. Then again, management refused to promote this individual because of her prior protected class EEO and NTEU activity, such as myself. On the other hand, it would have looked too suspicious to deny her the opportunity to compete and interview. In the alternative, the intent all along was to not select her, which was hurtful.

Why was I not afforded the opportunity to compete and interview the second time around? Reason being, an interview should not have taken place thirty days later. The entire competitive selection process involving SBB-SBL-2513 was scandalous! Everyone involved in the process should be held accountable for their actions, especially EEO. Their responsibility is to oversee that the process is fair, ensuring that *ALL* candidates are treated equitably. This was not done.

In saying so, an EEO Counselor is not supposed to score candidates in this process. I reiterate, their role should be a neutral one in the process. However, an EEO Specialist was in attendance, sharing notes with the rest of the panelists, erasing scores of some, in attempts to reward the candidate whom management preferred. These things in its entirety are illegal.

When EEO was questioned about the competitive selection process during mine and my coworker's hearings, this same Counselor boldly said, *"I was not aware that Alita's name appeared on the promotion certificate."* This is an untruth! As an EEO Counselor, she has an obligation to know! I say this with certainty because anytime positions are announced within the organization, the promotion certificate is sent to at least three entities. Those being: NTEU, EEO and the Territory Manager. Why?

According to established policy, this way *"supposedly"* protects everyone similarly situated, as well as to ensure the integrity of this process, leading to fairness and equality to all involved. If someone from EEO sits on the interview panel, surely they are aware of the candidates to be interviewed. Therefore, her statement bears no credibility either, same as the Territory Manager. I wholeheartedly assert that their actions caused a direct impact in the terms and conditions of my employment.

The Agency has maintained throughout that there was only one (1) GS 1101-11 Bankruptcy Specialist position available in Houston during this time period. Unfortunately for them, the documents that I present prove otherwise. You be the judge. Now what? I do not understand the rationale behind management not interviewing four candidates on the same day for one or more vacant positions! And yes, despite what management has sworn and testified to, one or more means just that, more than one!

This is why two (2) candidates were selected for this promotion, from this certificate. The Personnel specialist stated *"anytime interviews are held in promotional positions, if one person is interviewed, all candidates that are similarly situated deserve the same entitlement."* Subsequent the conversation, an EEO was filed the same day. What's ironic is that my evaluative appraisal was lowered, dated and presented to me on the same day that I informed my manager I'd be away from my workstation, meeting with an EEO Counselor. This was not happenstance. It was all planned by management in attempts to show me what would occur if I followed through with the filing of an EEO.

Obviously, my manager didn't care about zero tolerance. Then again, he has boldly admitted that he does not care who files complaints on him. With certainty, he states *"the complaints are not going anywhere."* For the most part, he's been absolutely correct. And he's not usually correct about any issue! Therefore, I'm left asking this question: *"Where is the justice?"* When my manager, was questioned about his involvement and my allegations, he said that *"his manager contacted him and advised him to only interview the first four candidates on the certificate."* Although he knew that to be wrong, he willfully chose to follow directives.

As federal employees and according to the Rules of Conduct, it's common knowledge that we have the responsibility, obligation and expectation to report any/all wrongdoing to our immediate managers or any management official. Now I'm really dumbfounded.

Why was my manager complicit throughout? And, why was he was in cahoots with his boss? Reason being, they consider themselves to be *"above the law, above reproach and not mere subordinates."* Their actions severely constitute interference and restraint, as it relates to the governing EEO laws.

The Territory Manager admitted that I was arbitrarily omitted from the competitive selection process because of my placement as the fifth BQ (best qualified) candidate on the selection certificate in error. He states that he intended all along to only interview the top four candidates. According to Personnel, *"a candidate's placement on the selection certificate has no bearing. If management chooses to interview, everyone listed must interview."* The cutoff score for consideration was **43.00**.

However, my score of ***44.77*** was well above the cutoff, but management disallowed me the opportunity to compete.

This is a prime example of how I was reprised against by management for filing complaints against my manager and the Agency. As a result of filing a complaint against this management official, my evaluative appraisal was lowered from 4.6 to 4.2, without any written negative documentation that warranted its lowering. Just think, these things happened to me and I am now cognizant of it. What about all of the unlawful things that occur on a daily basis at the IRS that we have no knowledge of!

The candidate in Houston who was eventually selected for this promotion, advised her manager that she would not be able to interview with the other candidates in August 2002 due to a prior engagement. Prior engagement? Therefore, her interview was rescheduled and conducted in September 2002. Despite the fact that I found this to be ridiculous, she was interviewed separately under the posted Vacancy Announcement number SBB-SBL-2513, with Houston being the only Post of Duty. The Vacancy Register, Ranking Spread Sheet and the Promotion Certificate all reflect three vacancies.

However, Personnel states that management could have interviewed as many as six candidates. If that's the case, why wasn't I interviewed? Although I asked, I know why. In an official IRS memo addressed to all employees from former Commissioner Mark W. Everson dated February 7, 2005: *"Reprisal against those who exercised their rights under applicable EEO laws will not be tolerated."*

The memo defines Reprisal as: *"any act of restraint, interference, coercion or discrimination against any person who has opposed the practices made unlawful by the governing EEO laws or because the person participated in the EEO process."* Another memo that was distributed (same day/same individual) via e-mail states *"the IRS is committed to creating and maintaining a work environment in which all employees are afforded the opportunities to succeed. I am committed to ensuring all employees the freedom to compete on a fair and level playing field with equal opportunity for competition."*

Was I afforded a fair and equitable opportunity based on the documents that I presented? Do you feel that I was denied the opportunity to compete based on the fact that I opposed management's wrongdoing? You are absolutely correct. Those are my sentiments exactly! The EEO complaint in Treasury defines *"Illegal Discrimination"* as an occurrence when an Employer intentionally treats one employee differently from another employee when the two are similarly situated and the treatment is based on protected group status (race, color, age, national origin, religion, sex, disability or EEO activity).

Similarly situated means that the employees occupy the same or similar positions, report to the same supervisor and the facts surrounding the action(s) are similar. Discrimination of this type is termed disparate treatment. It's funny how the Agency has the audacity to distribute correspondence of this nature via e-mail, but turns a deaf ear when presented with several examples of discrimination via EEO complaints that take place in the IRS offices on a daily basis, nationwide I'm sure. If you ask me, IRS administration should take a closer look at the managers and executive level managerial officials they rely on to do the right thing!

One of the best qualified candidates traveled from Austin to Houston for the interview but was not immediately selected for the GS 1101-11 promotion. During this time period, there were no other vacancies announced within this territory. Nevertheless, three months later, in December 2002, this same candidate was permanently promoted to a GS 1101-11 position in Austin under Vacancy Announcement number SBS-2S-206. This number is **FICTITIOUS** and does not exist on record with Personnel.

She advised another best qualified candidate that the only position she expressed interest in was the position that she interviewed for in Houston. She further states that her first-line manager *"arbitrarily"* approached her and advised her that she was being *"promoted to a GS 11Bankruptcy Specialist."* Now, I firmly believe that *"what you do in the dark will come to light."* It didn't dawn on me until years later, why that vacancy announcement was styled as such, one or more.

The Territory Manager's intent all along was to select one candidate from Houston, one from another office within the territory. He carried out his mission, in violation of policy and adverse to the rules and regulations set forth in promotional opportunities. What's so incredible about all of this is that there was no competitive selection process conducted that involved the Austin employee's promotion. This is another policy violation.

If anyone deserved a promotion, it should have been someone in Houston. At the very least, if management's intent was to select her, her post of duty should be Houston. As previously stated, she received permanent placement, whereas the Houston selectee only received temporary placement prior to being **DEMOTED** back to a GS 9

Bankruptcy Specialist, after having served in the position for almost two years. Aside from the absurdity, management's actions are once again discriminatory and disparate!

***** For the record, *"A single discriminatory act can affect an employee's ability to advance within the Agency, to receive promotions and to earn awards. Moreover, discrimination can debilitate an employee's self-confidence and sense of dignity."* *****

When the Territory Manager was finally questioned about the selection certificate and the competitive selection process, he also admitted that he did not return the document to Personnel for correction because of past problems with the Laguna office, citing the fact that he did not want to *"hold up"* the interview process in Houston. Since when did he care about Houston!!

Despite what he admitted to, the process was held up because everyone did not interview on the same day. If everyone had interviewed in August 2002, it would not have taken thirty days to select a candidate for the promotion. But, because the selectee interviewed later, the process was held up! So, there is absolutely no credibility in this management's official's response to this issue during questioning.

Again, common sense dictates that if a so-called error occurred on a document as important and critical as a selection certificate, personnel should have been notified. This individual found it needless to act on this because he intended to omit me from the process. If I was not worthy of consideration for this promotion, I would not have been identified as Highly Qualified/Best Qualified as rendered via personnel during ranking.

This was no error! Nevertheless, this management official took things upon himself to disregard my qualifications, whereas the other candidates received and benefited from an opportunity that I longed for, months to years later. Personnel states that it is management's responsibility to notify their office in the event an error occur. This was not done.

When I approached my manager about my interview, he was aware that I had been identified as best qualified. Therefore, **"I"** am the one who was deceived for several months and deliberately reprised against for opposing management's wrongdoing. It is my honest belief that the right to compete and interview in the competitive selection process is an opportunity that should be afforded to all interested parties. This is according to policy, rules, regulations and the Civil Service Reform Act (CSRA).

As the Territory Manager was being questioned during my EEO hearing, he advised everyone listening that, *"he did not know what the CSRA was, nor was he familiar with its policy."* How unlikely is that? He also admitted to not contacting personnel because he only "wanted" to interview the top four best qualified candidates. Wanted?

For reference sake, a person's WANTS have no place in this process. It should be about what's fair and equitable in the best interest of all qualified candidates! My DESIRE was to be a grade 11. I didn't get it did I? So, what sets this Territory Manager's wants and desires above my own? He is the authority figure in this matter and does not abide by what policy dictates. Keep reading, you'll understand where I'm going with this.

SEGMENT
FOUR

"WHEN
JUSTICE
FAILS"

CHAPTER XIV

Because I protected myself against management by filing complaints, I knew that I'd become a target, subjecting myself to acts of Retaliation/Reprisal and Harassment. My manager advised me constantly with a threatening tone saying, *"keep certain employees out of your work area or else"*, referring to only two of my peers in the adjoining group. These are the only two employees not allowed in his workgroup.

No matter how many times I mentioned to them that they were not wanted in his group, these employees knew that to be the only ones excluded from my work area was unfair and biased. Every employee in the department has visitors daily, although I am the only employee in his workgroup that this was demanded of. If for some reason he denies this, it will be one of many untruths spoken by this manager, once again!

When I spoke up by mentioning that his comments and requests constitute discriminatory disparate treatment, he would exclaim *"Just do it"*, as if he was speaking as a representative from NIKE! If I did not comply with his off the wall requests, he would write negative comments about me in narrative form when he shared reviews, and he'd talk about me openly to my peer group, in the work area. My manager was allowed to continue with his antics and to this day, it's still ongoing.

In May 2004, I was a witness in a coworker's EEO against the Agency, naming my manager also. The hearing was held on floor twelve in the EEO conference room. When I was summoned for testimony, I was unaware that my manager had been summoned too. Ironically, we took the same elevator and entered the office together. Since my testimony was rendered before his, he was asked to wait in the sitting room until which time he was called upon. Two days later, as I was leaving my workstation, I noticed my manager waiting to use the copier machine located just inside the exit door.

As I approached, he turned towards me, raised his fingers from a side holster as if he was pointing a gun and said *"POW, POW!* Any sane person knows that if you pull a gun on someone, you had better be prepared to use it. Otherwise, that same gun could end up down your throat! Let's just imagine the outcome if he had had a real gun. If so, I would have been dead, sleeping in my grave because my manager would not have fired only one round, he would have emptied the gun to obliterate me. This goes to show the level of contempt my manager has for me.

Nevertheless, I'm glad for two reasons. First, I'm glad that he didn't have a real gun. Second, I'm glad that the office was full of people, whereas someone would have been able to identify that gunslinger. On the other hand, knowing the employees as well as I do, they more than likely would have stated they did not witness a thing, although I'm lying there bleeding. Some people absolutely refuse to get involved. Why? Again I state, due to fear of reprisal from management. These acts are shameful but true!

In spite of this, I proceeded out of the door without saying a word. Shock is the very first emotion that overcame me, with anger following very close behind. The incident was immediately reported to a TIGTA agent in Washington, D.C., whereas I was advised that *"the matter could not be pursued because of the active EEO that was recently filed."* However, she asked that I contact her office once my EEO was resolved. The agent's response is contradictory to the RRA98 penalty guide. It states *"an employee who reports discrimination to TIGTA may file an EEO complaint also."* Nevertheless, she refused to help me. Therefore, management was allowed to continue harassing me without fear of retribution from the same inside entities who could have enforced restraint. Again I ask, what entity is willing to help? Why are employees advised to seek out these entities for assistance, but when the situation presents itself the doors are slammed in our faces?

This concept continues to baffle me year after year. In September 2004, my own EEO hearing against the Agency was held in the Houston office naming my manager and his superiors as the management officials, the Personnel Specialist from Laguna office, an EEO Counselor in Houston and several peers and coworkers as witnesses. Despite the fact that direct evidence was submitted as proof, despite the fact that Personnel testified to everything that was discussed via telephone regarding the illegal competitive selection process, despite the fact that the Administrative Judge cited in her decision that I had proven my case to be *"Prima Facie"*, this same judge ruled against me in favor of the Agency, stating *"I did not prove pretext existed."*

I am not a lawyer, yet I did my very best acting as Pro-se throughout the entire process. Because of her unfavorable ruling, my case was unjustifiably dismissed as "NO DISCRIMINATION" one month later. According to research, a case can be won on direct evidence alone. The direct evidence in my possession against the Agency was a slam dunk we all thought. But oh no, things were adverse to how the process should have gone. All was not fair in love and war! In other words, I disregarded the *"Rules of Engagement"* by stepping outside the box. As a result, I was disavowed immediately.

Upon receiving the Agency's decision weeks after the initial hearing, I persevered to the next step by exhausting all administrative remedies, filing an appeal to the EEOC, whereas the Administrative Judge's ruling was upheld. Despite this, I filed a Civil Suit in District Court in September 2005 as Pro-se. Needless to say, I didn't prevail in that arena either. Since when have you ever heard of a decision being rendered so swiftly? I know firsthand that Houston's EEOC judges are swamped and bombarded with busloads of complaints that are constantly and consistently filed, citing discrimination and several other serious allegations. My only guess is that the Agency wanted my case disposed of by any means necessary, and EEOC obliged them. It boggles the mind!

For years I wondered how I'd lost this case when in fact I presented such incriminating, direct evidence as proof. Subsequent the decision, I realized that I did not lose—a biased, unprecedented decision was rendered in favor of the Agency. Business as usual......

I'm a firm believer that you can't always expect people to do what YOU know to be right. When you have entities in place dutifully and exhaustingly working against the employee (grievant) in favor of the Agency, each time the employee ends up ass out! Remember, we're in a political season and elected constituents use this opportunity to call in markers! The correct reference is termed Quid Pro Quo or cronyism.

For those of you not familiar with the saying, it means *"if you scratch my back, I'll scratch yours."* I've been around the organization long enough to know when these things occur and have witnessed its occurrences too often. Shame on you, Uncle Sam!

After receiving notification of my case's dismissal, I attempted to settle within myself and accept the way that things were going to be. Not that I felt beaten down, unfortunately I began to believe that maybe my manager was correct when he mentioned years earlier, *"you can't win against the Agency."* He has said on several occasions that the entities in place to protect employees are *"sorry and worthless."*

He further states that *"NTEU is the laughing stock and no one wants the Vice-President to represent them because she has lost too many cases at their expense. The question remains: What expenses has he caused the Agency?"* If you mentioned the budget now, I'd understand.

It has been boldly noted in legal documents that he and his superiors have serious credibility issues and they have been referred to as liabilities. With that being said, what repercussions have any of them suffered as a result of the favorable ruling by the Administrative Judge, as it relates to a coworker's discrimination complaint? In a word, none to date. To the *"powers that be"*, if you've been informed that the system is flawed, fix it!

My manager went even further by saying that the President of NTEU *"just likes to hear herself talk and the Chief Steward is a joke."* He boasted by saying, *"NTEU knows not to mess with me, I'll put them in their place!"* Boy, it was extremely hard for me to maintain my composure and stop myself from laughing internally. Not because his comments were funny, I laughed hysterically because he sees fault in everyone except himself. The sad thing is the world is full of people just like him.

He knows that if anyone from the Union office had overheard his comments, he would have swallowed his tongue or instantly suffered from irritable bowel syndrome. You see, he pretends to be ill when the walls are closing in on him, mainly because he doesn't handle face-to-face confrontations very well. This is another documented proven fact.

What I find to be so incredulous about all of this is that everyone is aware that this individual was notorious for filing complaints against management prior to becoming one himself, after being *"kicked out"* of the manager's CADRE program, according to confidential sources. Now he has the audacity to criticize the same entities (NTEU/EEO) he scurried to for relief from the system that he now protects with utmost devotion!

Based on what I heard about his past, coupled with what I've witnessed and experienced firsthand, he's nothing close to being a model employee!

His insane comments have filtered out to the external community also. Sadly enough, I have witnessed and overheard his conversations via telephone when customers (taxpayers) called his office for assistance. If the taxpayer asked too many questions or perhaps asked for clarity about matters pertaining to their respective bankruptcy filings, he would become enraged. When arguments ensue with the customer, or if the customer is too persistent in questioning him, his favorite unprofessional lingo is, *"Whoa, Whoa, Whoa, come back down to earth!"* How much sense does that make?

Afterwards, he'd **DISCONNECT** the call saying *"they don't want to mess with me!"* Heaven forbid if the debtor calls back. If that happens, his attitude and demeanor is more irate than before. So much for professionalism! Better yet, so much for a *"Kinder, Friendlier IRS."* Why does everything with him turn into an argument if the parties involved disagree? I can only respond by saying, he gets upset and irritated because he knows that the customer is fully aware of the lack of knowledge he has on the topic that's being discussed. Getting angry and disconnecting the call is his way of *"saving face."*

Although there are some employees who are fearful to concur, they have witnessed and overheard some of the same conversations. It stands to reason that if you sit in such close proximity to his office, you are aware of these occurrences. For the record, I've even had to advise him to calm down in certain situations, where the debtor is involved. He perceived and accused the taxpayer of badgering him each time a call was transferred to his office. Just a reminder, the IRS's obligation is to provide quality customer service to America's taxpayer, as well as helping them to understand their tax obligations. Isn't that what the IRS Mission Statement reflects?

If this same manager observed us ill-advising the customer unprofessionally via statements during contact, or perhaps received complaints of unethical behavior, I can guarantee that our evaluative appraisal(s) would be impacted severely. However, he's responsible for evaluating employees on the level of quality customer service that's given to the debtor, but does not abide by the same policy when he himself fails so very badly in the same aspect, on its face.

CHAPTER XV

As for the internal community, my manager has on many occasions called several employees into his office to advise us exactly how the lawyers with District Counsel really feel about us, collectively and individually. He said, *"Those attorneys are prejudiced and have voiced their displeasure in having to work with the "Black Specialists" because we don't know our jobs."* He referred to them as being spoiled, obnoxious brats. He continued by saying that *"he has been told personally that the attorneys prefer to work with the WHITE employees only!"*

With the exception of one African American female attorney in that office, the makeup is comprised of Caucasian employees, males and females. And, ninety nine percent of the employees in my department is African American females, with one Caucasian male, one Hispanic male and one African American male. My manager said, *"He has received several unsatisfactory calls, emails and faxes about certain employees regarding their work ethic."*

In actuality, it's common knowledge that District Counsel is displeased with his performance as manager. In the aftermath, it's the employees who suffer the wrath because we report to him. These same attorneys have expressed discontent about his continual status as group manager after repeated complaints to his superiors about his work ethic and behavior. In his admission of these awful sentiments from Counsel, the real intent was to cause division and dissension between that office and ours. Sadly so his attempts proved successful. Even if his comments are true, a person's feelings should be taken into consideration before you set out to cause harm. Always remember, **words hurt. Once spoken, you cannot take back what's been said.** Although some apologies are rendered, sometimes that's not enough. The dye has already been cast!

Once my manager was notified via the Agency that my EEO had been dismissed, he called me into his office and said *"Aren't you glad that's over? I was worried about you, hoping that you did not commit suicide or something. All of that fighting is stressful."*

Why would he say something like that to an employee? With his warped thinking, he probably hoped that I would do just that to solve all of his problems! Management does not like the fact that I am opinionated, outspoken and assertive. At the same time, I'm dependable, loyal, dedicated and conscientious about my work ethic. Some managerial officials and their superiors operate on tyranny, domination, control and unethical methods for submission from employees. I thought we lived in a society governed by DEMOCRACY. On the contrary, SOME IRS managers in leadership positions rule the organization as a DICTATORSHIP. Subservience is demanded and their philosophy is, *"do what I say or else!"*

I make this comment with certainty because some employees are preyed upon and eventually become targets, for many different reasons. Some are made to feel like they are inadequate, some are verbally told they do not measure up and more times than not, they're talked down to, which contributes to low morale. For the most part, these are tenured employees with twenty plus years with the Service.

What's funny is that these are the same employees who received Exceed Fully Successful to Outstanding performance evaluations prior to my manager's arrival to this department. Now, all of a sudden some are inadequate, according to his verbal revelations. Isn't it incumbent upon one's immediate manager to coach and develop his/her employees? It stands to reason that if my manager was adequate in his role, employee inadequacies would be nonexistent, at the very least.

For example, many years ago a tenured employee walked off the job because of an unpleasant encounter with her manager, behind closed doors. This employee said that her manager shouted at her, threw papers to her across the desk and accused her of many unpleasant things, too numerous to name.

At the conclusion of the meeting, she tendered her resignation because she was berated, belittled and embarrassed. As it stands, she quit after having worked for this employer for almost twenty five years. At the time of her decision, I don't think she understood the ramifications of her actions. I do understand that she felt overwhelmed and reacted the best way she knew how, seeking relief from this manager's wrath. For many years, she exhausted all remedies in attempts at reinstatement, without success. Nevertheless, this was a no-win situation for both parties. So, where does the inadequacy lie?

As our group celebrated Christmas 2004, we were informed that our manager would be swapping with another group manager, that manager in turn would be assigned to our group. Typically, this swap out by management has been practiced before in the Service. Some employees in my group were elated to know that they would be given another opportunity to work with this female manager because of her calm, accepting nature. However, it didn't matter to me because she was just as corrupt and unethical in her methods as he. The only difference between the two of them is that she has enough sense to be subtle in her actions, whereas he's confrontational and his actions are blatant, wanton and without remorse.

Although one group was accepting of the swap out, the group that he was reporting to was not pleased at all to know who would report as their manager, after the holidays. Reason being, they had heard horror stories about his management style and they knew that things were about to change considerably. His reputation as a manager preceded him. We have been at odds since April 2002, from the moment that he wrote me up and accused me of not following a directive.

One day, several of my peers and I held a round table discussion in the conference room during lunch, whereas his management style was the topic of discussion. These employees were aware that this individual had lowered several of our evaluations unjustifiably, and others were aware of the derogatory comments that he'd made in group meetings, etc. The only thing I advised them of is that they will not encounter problems unless/until they disagree with him, on whatever topic, business or personal. Since given the opportunity, I was not going to sugarcoat and intentionally lead them to believe that everything was going to be a bed of roses. *"If you sleep in a rose garden with the Devil, you wake up with thorns!"* And, my opinion was rendered only because it was solicited.

It has been said that *"you don't know what a person is going through until you experience it yourself."* Surely, his bewildered employees were about to experience some of the same things some of us already had. With the exception of one employee, the group was submissive and he savored that. As soon as he reported to the office, his first task was to deal with evaluative reviews and annual appraisals. Because the prior (female) manager was not managing effectively by reviewing her employees' work product on a regular basis, the evaluative appraisals were "rolled over" for each employee, meaning that their exorbitant, questionable numerical ratings remained the same as the prior year due to the lack of documentation in their personnel files. This was a good thing for them because some received monetary awards once again when they weren't entitled to one the year before.

Naturally, I thought this to be a bad business decision but understood that it had to occur according to policy. Why hold the employee(s) accountable for a managers' irresponsibility? But others similarly situated has always been held to higher standards with greater expectations under certain managers' leadership. Some of us were recipients of negative write ups and lowered evaluations, although our group is the group that produced quality work on a consistent basis. In the interim, the adjoining group of employees coasted and enjoyed benefits under her regime year after year. This infuriated my former manager to no end! By him having to rollover these employees, he openly and verbally berated them to anyone who'd listen, which is highly unethical. As if he's a Rhodes Scholar!

This manager told me how his boss (Territory Manager) openly ridiculed this female manager during conference calls, with all of the managers within the territory listening in on their extensions, little did she know. Once the call was disconnected, she became the butt of all of their jokes, each of them snickering about her for months, with the Territory Manager as ring leader! My manager said that, *"he always met his deadlines because his butt is too small to be getting chewed out by his boss."* He said, *"She has plenty cushion back there so she can take it!"*

When I alerted him that those matters were private and should not be discussed with me, he kept right on with the ridicule. I'm sure he's envious because some employees actually liked her. It didn't take a rocket scientist to figure out how those same employees felt about him. Obviously, his respect for his colleague was minimal, if any at all. I remain cognizant of the fact that if he felt so comfortable talking about a colleague to me, surely he talked about me and my peers to others similarly situated, as well as to other levels of management.

CHAPTER XVI

It didn't take long for him to exert his authority over certain employees in his new group. He would call them to his office and accuse them of almost anything, just to get a rise out of them. Often times than not, he would ridicule them in the form of negative documentation, as well as verbally in the work area. He took this position against one employee in particular because she was not afraid to rebut his attempt at domination. When management takes arbitrary actions against this employee, she counteracts by soliciting assistance from NTEU/EEO. He absolutely resents that and has in turn become a force to be reckoned with! Management was overwhelmed and knew of no way to stop her. Therefore, they trumped up all sorts of untruths in attempts to tarnish her reputation.

It's a known fact that this employee had to go it alone because some of her peers were in fear of reprisal from their manager, if they stood with her. Several of them turned deaf ears and actually hid in their work spaces, hoping that he would not target them. You can run, but you can't hide! It's a shame to admit this, but management uses coworkers and intentionally intimidates others, using coercion as a weapon to make false statements under oath, against those who are disliked by the staff. With that being said, this manager has not been reprimanded for his actions nor has he been penalized for his devious acts.

Because she is not afraid to exercise her protected rights, management is not beneath lying on her. With the exception of present company, there is only one other employee within the department who is not afraid to speak up. Management has everyone else terrified to even speak on anything considered to be abnormal in the Houston office. If the employees refuse to conform, their annual appraisals are lowered, some will receive negative write ups, some will be reported to TIGTA for investigation AND some are/have been subjected to audits of their personal tax returns—becoming collateral damage. If I am not mistaken, the auditing of taxpayer returns is a supposed *"random"* selection by the computers. Let it be known, *"if an employee files a grievance or EEO against the Agency, you'll find out where you stand in a relatively short period of time."*

Alternatively, adverse actions are taken against certain employees at the behest of senior executive level management through directives to first level managerial officials because of the dislike for the employee(s), and because of the employees' participation in prior protected class EEO activity. This is termed retaliatory animus, leading to discrimination, which is a policy violation.

One morning in particular, I heard this same employee scream, *"Somebody help me, somebody help me. I need a witness!"* Immediately and without hesitation, we rushed to her aid. Before I could get there, several other coworkers escorted her outside to safety. As I turned the corner, her manager was standing inside of his office door smirking and commenting, *"where is the parade?"* I passed him without saying anything as he stood there laughing. How insensitive. Moments later, it was told to me that he had spoken untruths to her about the work procedures. As she attempted to ask for clarity, he threatened her. Typical. He has a way of trying to make employees feel small because of his very own shortcomings or should I say insecurities! *"He who laughs, laughs last."*

It's as if management is happiest when the employees are at their lowest point. In the event you become vulnerable, they will pounce on you like a hawk after its prey. Then, they will stop at nothing to keep you under their dominance and control by overexerting their authority. In a word, your wings will be *"clipped"* rendering you immobile. Shocking huh? If your wings are clipped, you cannot rise above the clouds. And, that's management's objective, to prevent this from happening.

This wasn't the first time that something of this nature occurred between the two of them in his office. On another occasion, he called this same employee to the office in attempts to discuss work procedures. That's his method of operation. Since his explanation differed from the Internal Revenue Manual, this individual disagreed with his rationale. That is when he became upset! The employee solicited help from a member of her peer group, asking her to interpret for the manager exactly what the manual stated.

The manager interjected and threatened his employee by saying, *"you don't want to get involved in this do you?!"* Instantly, she turned to leave, in fear of her manager's threats if she sided with her coworker against him. For the record, it's not about taking sides, it's about what's true and correct according to policy.

Management's offensive behavior, coupled with the repeated verbal abuse and sabotage is used on some as a form of *"bullying"* in attempts to force employees to surrender against their will. It's been said that *"Black"* women are often treated as inferior, causing them to be low-performers in the workplace. If you ask me (and I'm sure that several will agree), some managers themselves feel inferior to *"strong"* women, no matter their nationality. That's the contributing factor as to why women are subjected to many acts of REPRISAL more so than men. In a word, men are respected automatically within the organization , whereas women have to work harder to garner respect.

In part, women fall short of the mark daily based on disturbing comments that are often spoken or acts that are implied. That's unfortunate because I find a lot of women to be quite intelligent. Although some females have attained several years of undergraduate/post graduate studies, some of their male counterparts barely graduated high school. Aside from that, males advance up the corporate ladder effortlessly. It's as if management closes their eyes, throw a dart and the male employees' name magically appear. Aha, you're promoted. On the other hand, the female more qualified candidate is left scratching her head. How could this be? I declare, some males in high ranking positions leave a lot to be desired. Having said that, pay parity still exists between men and women. And, I'm sure this exists across a broad spectrum in that many employers are reluctant to admit.

What happened to life, liberty and the pursuit of happiness as afforded to us all via the Constitution? These freedoms are non-existent within this organization. This established right along with many others are frowned upon if you're found to be too assertive! Is there such a thing? Better yet, you had better not assert yourself against management. If so, you'll face the Agency's wrath in a swift kick. But, if you're submissive and succumb to management's tactics, you'll forever be welcomed into their clique.

As a reward, you might find yourself at the *"Head of the Class"* regardless of your qualifications and job knowledge. An individual/employee should not be beaten up, beaten down and made to feel less than human because of the differences of opinions that they possess. Just think how unbalanced this world would be if everyone was alike. **OMG!**

PREAMBLE

"We the people of the United States, in order to form a more perfect Union, establish Justice, insure domestic Tranquility, provide for the common defense, promote the equal Welfare, and secure the blessings of Liberty to ourselves and our Prosperity, do ordain and establish this Constitution for the United States of America."

CHAPTER XVII

Memory takes me back to an occasion when all of the employees in my department attended a mandatory training class concerning the upcoming changes in work procedures. The classroom instructor was a female manager from another locale within the territory. Each day before class, she conducted an impromptu question and answer session about celebrities. One morning, a male coworker raised the question about *"feasibility."* This was the absolute wrong thing to do. By this time, the former male manager had been reassigned back to my group.

When a female employee interjected, commenting about feasibility previously being referred to as *"disposal income"* before her manager's word change, this classroom instructor (managerial official) shouted, *"Do you need a timeout?!"* She asked this same question three times. I thought that to be excessive, but then again my opinion has never mattered to management, that is. Each time the question was repeated, the employee's response was, *"No ma'am, thank you."* Shortly thereafter, this instructor interjected by saying, *"I will not tolerate disrespect of anyone in this room!"* Question: Why was the employee's comment considered to be disrespectful? I don't believe the comment infuriated this manager. However, I do believe the employee voicing the comment infuriated her. And, I arrive at this assessment based on the unfavorable comments that have been said by management to others across the territories, as it relates to certain employees in the Houston office.

The class consisted of about twenty five employees, including both managers in Houston. I was puzzled and didn't understand why this was happening. As she was instructing, this official chimed in saying, *"now you're finally going to be doing the jobs that you are paid to do, despite the fact that some of you don't have college degrees!"* Excuse me?! We had only been introduced to her that morning. So, when had she formed that assessment of us? For her to boldly state this, she would have had to talk with her colleagues and other levels of management about the employees in Houston. Otherwise, how does she know who does/does not have degrees?! Some of the employees in attendance may have more credentials than her. It would be interesting to know her educational background!

A college degree is a college degree. It does not mean that you're smarter, nor does it mean you earned that degree. I've read about college students circumventing school policy by taking entrance exams (SAT's) for their friends to ensure acceptance, as well as attending classes for other individuals to guarantee passing grades in certain courses, all the while they're being paid enormous sums to defraud colleges and universities across the nation, just to prove to others that they have a college degree. And, this happens more times than have been reported on a national level. This is waste, fraud and abuse. When this happens, the *"degree"* isn't earned legitimately. However, the one benefit is to be in possession of a degree sets you apart from most. If we all searched our family tree, I'm sure that we'll discover that some relatives within our sect lack degrees but have brilliant minds and are exceptional nonetheless! So, I'm left asking myself why did she feel the need to express such an off the wall sentiment?

A few days later, the interrogated employee was written up and threatened with a five day suspension because of what management said transpired during the training session. The Territory Manager received notification from his managers alerting him to the fact that the employee hollered, jumped up and voiced all sorts of un-pleasantries in response to the instructor's very direct interrogation. In a word, they lied! However, the employee filed a grievance with NTEU same day and her complaint proceeded to arbitration. Naturally, I documented exactly what transpired, therefore forwarding my written statement as evidence. In the interim, my recollection of that morning overwhelmingly contradicted management's malevolent untruths! How odd is that?

Without a doubt, these managers had formed a conspiracy against her. Each knew that their statements were false, but they agreed to uphold each other's wrong doing. Always remember, the choices we make today affect our tomorrows. NTEU utilized me as a witness during arbitration which was fortunate for the employee but unfortunate for the Agency. From an ethical standpoint, I could not allow anything adverse to happen to her when in fact I (and others) knew the truth. Both of us are fully aware that *"not everyone would have stepped up to the plate like I did."* And, that was proven. Everyone else stuck their noses in the sand. Clearly, management was wrong. They usually are.

The employee won her case in arbitration. Therefore management, with much reluctance was required to rescind the negative write up that was intended for her. By having to do so, they searched elsewhere in attempts to bring her down. To make things absolutely clear, contrary to popular belief, we are our brother's keeper!

If you ask this individual how long she's had to fight to keep her employer off her, the response would be since 1991, half of her career with the IRS. That's unfortunate, but serves as proof that the Agency will stop at nothing, in attempts to get their employees to bow down. After management received notification that she prevailed against them, the telephones started ringing, mine particularly. Hours later, my manager angrily contacted me by phone stating, *"Ms. Carter, I need to see you!"* Based on the tone in his voice, he was furious. As soon as I stepped to the door, he chimed in by nastily asking, *"why are you always rescuing her?!"* I'm a firm believer that we should be nice to people because you never know who you'll need to be there to rescue you. Philosophy dictates that the bridge we burn may be the same bridge we may need to cross someday.

According to this employee, prior to this individual's status as manager in Insolvency, he'd make personal trips to the downtown office to visit her on government time. (This is what's considered to be waste, fraud and abuse of the system). Notably so, several employees witnessed him sitting in her work area for hours on end, with his legs crossed, propositioning her for dates. He'd even call each year on her birthday to express *"Happy Birthday"* sentiments.

When she reminded him that he was a married man, his response was that he and his wife have an *"open relationship."* Why should anyone have to remind someone of their marital status? She refused his advances by advising him that *"she does not date married men."* Once she *"spurned his advances"*, she suddenly became his bitter enemy! Prior to this occurrence, she actually considered him to be a friend. *"Don't criticize and speak evil about each other, dear brothers. If you do, you will be fighting against God's law of loving one another, declaring it is wrong. But your job is not to decide whether this law is right or wrong, but to obey it. Only HE who made the law can rightfully judge among us. HE alone decides to save us or destroy. So, what right do you have to judge or criticize others?"* **James 4:11-12**

CHAPTER XVIII

One day several employees were discussing a group meeting that had been held in the conference room. It was stated that this manager openly and verbally attacked the employee when she asked questions about the work process he was attempting to explain. It's common knowledge that he doesn't like questions directed to him. He took her persistence as a personal attack and advised the employees in attendance to, *"leave the room"*, stating *"it's going to be me and her, leave us in the room alone!"*

At the time the comment was made, the employee had stepped out momentarily. It was said that he used hand gestures to the group, demonstrating or insinuating that he wanted to fight her fist to fist. When the employees refused to leave, he became upset with them, challenging them to a duel, one on one. He said, *"come on, come on, I'll take all of you one by one!"* Again, the malevolence of his acts shows the mentality of some of the individuals whom the IRS employ and eventually elevate to managerial positions.

Despite the fact that NTEU was present and advised this manager that his comments were inappropriate, he continued with his antics, disregarding NTEU's assessment of the situation. I shudder to think what would have happened had NTEU not been there! I suppose that the employees' initial emotion was shock, considering what they had just witnessed. Once more, the employee filed a complaint in attempts to protect herself from this manager. When she alerted the *"powers that be"* via e-mail about her situation, again upper management turned a deaf ear.

Instead of reaching out to assess what they had been made aware of, the advice that she received from senior executive level officials was to *"cease and desist"* with the e-mails because they were clogging their computers. Furthermore, management advised her that she would be subject to disciplinary actions if she refused to follow that directive! Imagine that. It is my belief that the computers wouldn't be clogged if *"some"* executives addressed the urgent need for employee assistance before things spiraled out of control.

This manager has stated in sworn affidavits that *"this individual needs medical assistance for her bi-polar condition."* It has never been documented by medical personnel that she suffers from any kind of disorder. This is what has been said about her to others in attempts to ruin her credibility. Nevertheless, it has been documented in court records that SOME Agency officials have serious credibility issues. If you ask me, he needs to seek assistance for his narcissistic behavior. Several employees have witnessed him sitting or standing in his office using hand gestures, as if he's conversing with someone when it's clearly visible no one's there. And, he's not speaking to anyone through a headset either. To the medical community, he might be characterized as schizophrenic or one who exhibits behavioral personality disorders!

Because of my association/affiliation with certain employees, my manager has referred to us as the ***"THREE MUSKETEERS."*** Reason being, each of us have strong personalities and we each have opposed management's wrongdoing on more than one occasion by participating in the complaints process, etc. For these reasons, we have been labeled as troublemakers by management. Notably so, we are the *"three employees"* who stand together against wrongdoing. The other employees are not feared because they do not pose a threat to management whatsoever. It's safe to say that some have been programmed and have conformed out of fear of reprisal. Anytime management saw us together, we were constantly watched like paparazzo infringing upon the lifestyles of celebrities. We thought their actions were awfully peculiar—no one else within the department was watched so closely. Little does management know, they catapulted us to power without much difficulty.

My manager admitted to some of my peers that, *"Alita is spoiled, always wanting things her way. I'm going to tear her playhouse down!"* When he was questioned about his own ASININE comments, once again his response was *"I didn't say that."* These repeated denials were becoming incredulous.

Honestly, he reminds me of someone on the popular sitcom whom we all know.

In August 2005, the Chief of Advisory/Insolvency/Quality (AIQ) visited the Houston office to meet with and discuss upcoming changes, as well as to address employee concerns. There were about ten employees in attendance, myself included, absent management. Three employees' jobs were in jeopardy, facing possible layoffs. A clerical employee informed this managerial official that she had recently received a Reduction in Force letter (hereinafter RIF), advising her that her position was going to be abolished. So, she sought instructions from him as to what she could do to possibly prevent this from happening. His response was not readily given, but he did respond to her questioning sometime thereafter. Months later, this employee was dismissed. She was an African American, GS 7 clerk with tenured status.

A GS 9 employee in receipt of the RIF letter was forced to retire, while a GS 11 employee was arbitrarily rolled over from one grade series to another, without the benefit of having to compete for her professional position in the department. I smell another policy violation! Although this employee's (former) position was abolished, the grade series was not. Why wasn't she reassigned to another locale within the same series, and allowed to continue working in the Houston office in order to avoid relocation? I've seen this happen all the time. However, she was rolled over from that grade series to another, without the benefit of having to interview and compete for her professional position within the department. And, her job duties were totally different from the position she now holds.

Hence, her appointment *"blocked"* someone else's appointment from GS 9 to GS 11 in Houston. This was done by design. Furthermore, this individual lacked the required Knowledge, Skills, Abilities and Other (KSAO) characteristics required for this position. In other words, she had to be trained, whereas the GS 9 Specialists had time in grade, as well as the required KSAO's for elevation to the next phase in their career. As a form of punishment, we were overlooked again intentionally. It can be said that this GS 11 employee is one whom management favors because of her quiet, unsuspecting nature.

To compound matters, there were several GS 7 employees in the Austin and Phoenix offices who were recipients of RIF letters also. In order to protect them from layoff, the Territory Manager arbitrarily moved them from their *"clerical GS 592"* positions to paraprofessional (GS 1101-9) Bankruptcy Specialist positions/promotions, hereby exempting them and bypassing the competitive selection process for promotions. If memory serves me correctly, these individuals were Caucasian and Hispanic.

Unfortunately, the clerical employee here was not afforded this luxury because she worked in this office and because of her race, I presume. She became collateral damage. The Houston employees suffered a different fate, when in fact the promotions were for jobs announced here, according to Personnel.

Let's be real people. Just because you may be the apple of management's eye, what's wrong is wrong. Nevertheless, I place no fault with these employees one bit. If someone offered me a promotion (under the table) or perhaps moved *"heaven and earth"* for me to remain on the payroll (under the table), I would probably be accepting also. Yet, I would always watch my back. You have become indebted to the Agency and the balance can never be repaid. Your thoughts are no longer your own, you jump when they order you to or else! This is also a policy violation in the terms and conditions of one's employment.

When I returned to work the next day, my manager called me to the office and angrily asked, *"why are you always involved in mess?!"* Here we go again! I immediately knew what he was referring to but was shocked that he had the audacity to ask that question. He said, *"I know who was in attendance and I know who voiced concerns!"* That's when he said that his superior told him the names of all the employees who were present. I could have responded by asking him the same question. He and his superiors are the creators of the hostile work environment in which we work! But, I reserved my comments for a later date. This was a retaliatory step instituted by the department's Director as a form of intimidation and harassment.

CHAPTER XIX

Because of lengthy illnesses, coupled with family issues that required immediate attention, my manager was out of the office for an extended period of time. Therefore, a female (Hispanic) manager was sent to the Houston office from Austin to take over the managerial duties for our group, along with managing her current group of employees offsite. She reported to my department on January 9, 2006, acting as a covert agent with a planned agenda as instructed by the Agency.

As soon as she entered Insolvency's door, it didn't take long for anyone to ascertain that she was not a happy camper. Her sharp, wrinkled facial expression led me to believe she'd sucked a barrel of persimmons or something closely related earlier on. When the manager failed to identify herself, a coworker asked her name and a follow up question as to why she was here. Only then, that's when she identified herself as being from another office within the territory.

A coworker asked, *"Are you here to replace a Houston manager?"* Her chilling response was *"no, I'm here to handle some administrative things for the group's manager."* She in turn asked, *"On which end does the group start?"* We concluded that she was here to conduct reviews.

The group consisted of about ten employees at the time of her arrival, with a few employees sitting in different areas within the office. This manager began by approaching employees' workstations, asking them to access certain computer programs, so as to gauge their job knowledge and how they performed specific job duties. On her very first day she reviewed three of my peers. I was not interviewed until two days later. When she approached my workstation, I felt a cold draft. This manager has a way of making you feel uncomfortable to be in her presence. No one should have that kind of an effect on you in your own home!

Understandably, she was only with me momentarily. I guess she felt my draft too. To my surprise and disbelief, she held conversations with a male employee in the group, stating to him *"some employees are on board and some employees need lots of help."* She went on to say, *"I've heard about these employees in Houston, they leave a lot to be desired!"* She was unaware that her comments were overheard. I was in the next cubicle discussing a business matter with a peer when these insults rolled off her tongue. For her to say these things to anyone, let alone someone in this office, was totally unprofessional and unethical! The male employee interjected by informing her that, *"there are some good, hardworking employees in Houston."* I was so proud of him at that moment because it was as if he was defending my honor, although no names were called. It would have been priceless to get a glimpse of her facial expression after being advised of that!

From the onset, her actions were inappropriate. For instance, when she sent e-mails to the group or perhaps called the Houston office from Austin, her tone was antagonistic and threat provoking. Her detail called for a weekly commute from Austin to Houston. When she traveled back to her assigned locale to work, she solicited information from squealers within the group to keep her abreast of everyone's activity, especially the ones she disliked. What's disturbing is that she didn't have to twist anyone's arms for bits and pieces of information. Not everyone wants to be the teacher's pet. Some people have scruples!

Quite naturally, I alerted NTEU about her comments and a meeting was scheduled to discuss the statements that disturbed us. I was present at the meeting because I documented what I overheard, in the event that she had a sudden case of amnesia like her counterpart in the other office. When I read back to her what I overheard her say, she did not deny anything. How admirable of her! She could be characterized and labeled as many things but at least she did not lie! I can respect that. As I was reading, she had this blanket expression on her face while she fidgeted profusely in her chair. You see, some of us here have encountered so much controversy and adversity in Houston, we've learned to document everything for future reference to protect ourselves. This manager's explanation to NTEU was that *"there's too much work in Houston and she's witnessed too much socializing in the office."* I interjected by asking, *"Are the employees in Austin chained to their desks?"* Her response was *"no, they work though."* Could it be that she was insinuating that the employees in Houston are non-performers?

To the best of my memory, unless things have changed considerably, Austin has less inventory, less courts and more employees to get the job done, with smaller manageable courts. On the flip side, Houston has more courts, larger courts and fewer employees per team than Austin. However, the Houston office is faced with greater expectations and demands to meet exorbitant deadlines. It is a known fact that some Austin employees have been the recipients of permanent promotions, despite the fact that no announced vacancies existed that warranted placement. Far be it from that, some of these same employees are exempted from undergoing the competitive selection process altogether, based on personal favoritism by management. There are several employees in the Austin office who fall under this criteria.

During this meeting I asked the manager, *"Why does she solicit help from selective employees in the group versus total group involvement?"* Instinctively, she responded by saying, *"Alita, you don't talk to me, therefore I don't talk to you."* She went on to say, *"Some employees have sought assistance from me, these are the employees whom I gravitate towards."* No, she gravitates toward certain employees because they bring bones to her about other employees, making her a willing participant in the nonsense.

Based on what's told to her about certain employees, she prepares unsavory documentation to present to them when she returns to the Houston office, advising them of their right to seek union representation. Her actions are disparate and discriminatory because she listens to employee complaints of others before investigating and researching the matter, whatever it may be, on her own. This is a travesty of justice!

I saw firsthand how she created and contributed to the already Hostile Work Environment. She accepts the complaints of some, depending on how she felt about certain employees, you knew what to expect! Human nature dictates that people report others and not themselves. If I were a manager, I would be compelled to take a close look at employees who constantly report nasty comments to management about the workgroup. These employees are DANGEROUS. They consistently *"throw others under the bus"* so that their own wrongdoing won't be exposed! Better yet, some serve as liaisons for the manager(s) in his/her absence. Makes you wonder what other kind of incentives are imposed upon them for their acts of *"loyalty"* to the organization via plea bargains! More times than not, these same employees are GUILTY themselves.

Despite the negativity, it's awfully peculiar how this female manager sees fit to *"break bread"* with her employees during Happy Hour, but from 9:00am-5:00pm their heads are placed in the guillotine, often times for reasons as minute as hers and others disdain for them. It's funny how she drinks socially and uncontrollably with the workgroup after hours but does not treat them with an ounce of dignity and respect during business hours! Ponder that......

Prior to our meeting, this manager approached several of us in the work area and asked point blank, *"why do you all entertain this individual? You should just walk away from her when she approaches."* The manager said, *"This employee doesn't know me, I'll step to her!"* She was so angry she could have shattered glass with her bare hands. I was present when the manager voiced these sentiments and I was flabbergasted! Again I ask, was she insinuating that she'll fight the employee if pushed come to shove? I took it to mean that she'll be the one person to finally put her this employee in her place, since other management officials were obviously afraid to discipline her or had not been successful in their attempts to discipline her! Her insensitive comments rendered me speechless, and that's a rarity.

One of the employees present, (very carefully) advised this manager that she would not walk away from anyone as they're speaking because it's rude. The employee asked, *"How would you like for someone to walk away from you as you're speaking?"* The manager abruptly turned to leave without a response. When her comments were relayed to the employee, she immediately reported the incident to EEO, in attempts to shed light on the manager's hidden agenda. It was clear to us that this manager was acting on things that she had been told about this employee. The subjected employee was not even assigned to her group, so there was no need for manager/employee interaction between the two of them.

According to my male group manager, when this same female manager instructed a bankruptcy training class in Phoenix once upon a time, she was the laughing stock and the butt of daily jokes. He stated that he received calls from several of the employees in that training class advising him that this manager never knew the answers to the questions that were asked. Instead, she would call her boss (Territory Manager) several times a day for him to help bail her out. I don't understand why my manager insists that employees nationwide call him to keep him abreast of what's going on in certain locales. I could ask him, *"Why are you always involved in mess?"* Does he think that he's Mr. Popularity or something? It's true that's he's well known by many within the Houston community and abroad, both internally and externally but not for the reason(s) he thinks!

Without a doubt, she has evaluated employees' progress and has on occasion lowered some of them unjustifiably in Houston, due to bias and has perhaps increased some that actually warranted lowering. Upon presenting an employee with her mid-year during the evaluative period, this manager advised the employee, *"if you don't approve of this document that I'm giving you, take it to the Union, I don't care!"* Where do they get these managers from? Do they crawl from under rocks or something! We all know that some things are better left unsaid. A person should not always verbalize what they're thinking. Sometimes silence is golden.....

At the conclusion of Revenue Officer training in August 2006, this female manager addressed the class with closing remarks. Along with the Houston employees, there were other attendees present from Austin, Las Vegas and Phoenix. She opened up by saying, *"the training material that we were introduced to during that week will be used as an evaluative tool in future mid-years and performance appraisals."* She boldly exclaimed, *"if the employees whom she manage has "no problem" receiving all three's (3=fully successful) in an evaluative period, she'll be happy to oblige them!"*

My manager was seated alongside her (looking around the room acting like a puppet) while the puppet master stood, pulling his strings. Although he was amazed and awestruck by her dastardly comments, he refused to chastise her by remaining silent throughout. *"Unspoken words carry as much weight as verbalized ones."* To reiterate, although he said nothing, her sentiments were his also. I was not the least bit surprised by either of their actions. When my manager should speak out, he practices silence. Alternatively, when he should be silent, he goes overboard. Typical.

comment. However, since she considered her Austin group to be superior, one can only conclude that her disgust was directed towards the Houston group of employees only. As I allowed my mind to drift back, I distinctively recall the Director of AIQ saying, *"The Houston employees have quality issues."* For this reason and more, he wholeheartedly believes that we should not be entitled to advancement within this organization. Better yet, my manager advised an EEO investigator that, *"the Houston office have filed too many EEO complaints, as being the reason why "no employee in this department will ever be promoted."* Again, IRS administration should be concerned with the level of egregiousness in these matters versus placing emphasis on management's displeasure with the number of complaints that's filed here!

CHAPTER XX

I am privy to information that my manager is not aware of. His colleague has openly voiced her displeasure with the pay parity that exists between the Houston and Austin offices. Houston's locality pay is higher than most areas. Therefore, the employees here earn more than their counterparts nationwide. To compound things, this manager went a little further saying *"that she is upset because her colleagues in Houston earn more than she does."*

It's funny how the employees here are always being counseled about *"consistency, professionalism and dissension"*, when there are managers within this territory/office who obviously envy and literally despise one another. Is it safe to say that they do not work and play well together? If managers display a lack of respect within their own sect, how could I possibly expect to be treated with common courtesy and decency as a member of the workgroup? Because of the aforementioned and other reasons, their actions alone have created the abnormality and dysfunction abroad. If it's true that managers lead by example, then that explains why the *"flavor"* of the work environment is indeed malevolent!

I was told that during a group meeting, she verbally informed her employees exactly how much income the managers in Houston earn in relation to hers. She approached the bulletin board in the room and actually wrote down her colleagues' salaries, for all to see, versus her own income. This constitutes disclosure and is highly unethical and unlawful.

The employees from Houston were paid travel and per diem to attend this meeting in Austin, supposedly to discuss the Survey 2007 results. According to my peers, she never even touched on the survey results. She used that session to express her dissatisfaction with certain employees, as well as to verbalize those things she has wanted to say since her detail began. This is what's referred to as waste, fraud and abuse. Doesn't she know that what's done in Vegas does not necessarily stay in Vegas! Oh well, she'll find out at a later date.

Don't you think that if I was always involved in mess (as I have been accused of by my manager), I would have made it my mission to inform him that he/his salary was being discussed/disclosed unlawfully, as well as the level of disrespect that he has garnered from his own colleague. After everything that I've been subjected to over the years, I respected his feelings. Is this ludicrous or what? Despite what some of you are willing to believe, I do have a heart.

In the alternative, he (and others) should learn to practice and foster the same respect whereas employees' feelings are concerned. Just think, if she discloses this kind of information about management salaries to her disinterested employees, I shudder to think what taxpayer information has been disclosed in unrelated matters. I cannot think of enough adjectives to describe her actions. The words willful, intentional and egregious stand out in my mind.

One day I witnessed her *"very nasty"* approach to a coworker when she presented the employee with the monthly docket for consolidation to District Counsel and the trustees' representative prior to an upcoming court hearing. One of our peers advised the manager that this responsibility *"needed to be rotated because she herself had had the responsibility for several months and had become overwhelmed."* Actually, this employee told her manager that she was not going to do it anymore! Isn't this commonly referred to as insubordination? For the record, it depends on how management felt about particular employees. These things shouldn't apply, but it does. However, the insubordinate employee and her manager were very close buddies, leading her to demand and receive special treatment from this manager.

Moments later, the manager reassigned the duties to an employee similarly situated, one whom she despises. The employee in turn did not refuse this assignment. She only inquired as to why she was receiving the docket at such a late date because the confirmation hearing was fast approaching. Needless to say, the manager became infuriated at this employee by openly exclaiming, *"I'm not going to allow you to cause dissension in the work area!"* What's with not being able to ask questions of management? Why are they so defensive? How is it that this employee's question constitutes dissension? Without provocation, the manager turned on me! What had I done?

She walked away and approached my manager in his office, angrily advising him that I was sitting in her work area. According to him, she demanded that he *"come witness the employee!"* What had she done? I was sitting in his work area, not hers, innocently attaching prints that I had just retrieved from the copier. Once he approached, I was returning to my workstation as we passed one another in the aisle. Upon returning to my desk, the phone rang. It was my manager summoning me to his office. When I entered, he demanded that I close the door and immediately asked, *"What's going on?"* I was perturbed because I had done nothing that would warrant a counseling session.

His colleague complained that I was sitting in her area and witnessed the exchange that had just transpired. There was no exchange. For the record, I wasn't sitting in her area. The seat that I utilized while I worked was assigned to my manager's group. What was her motive? Far be it from that, my manager demanded that *"I stay away from that work area. He exclaimed, just do what I say and stay away!"* I asked, *"Why do I have to stay away if my work takes me there?"* He did not respond right away. As I prepared to exit his office, he mumbled the words *"because I said so!"*

Days later, I was summoned to his office again about this same matter. He said, *"You should get tired of having your name linked to hers, that's not good!"* He referred to this employee as an *"IDIOT"* and boldly stated, *"I don't care if you tell her what I said!"* Those inflammatory comments infuriated me to no end and I advised him that I would not stand there any longer while he ridiculed and belittled her or anyone else, for that matter! As expected, I was secretly reported to TIGTA and investigated, I assert because of my known affiliation with certain employees whom management despise!

As soon as I left his office, I went outside to catch my breath and try to recover from what transpired between my manager and me. After bumping into the employee who was the topic of discussion, and after she witnessed my demeanor and facial expression, she knew right away that something terrible had taken place. When I relayed his comments to her, she filed another EEO complaint against both managers. She was well within her right to do so! When the EEO Counselor questioned my manager about these comments, he stated *"I did not say that."* Here we go again. With much reluctance, he later recanted.

In order to overshadow his wrongdoing, he advised the counselor that this individual and I have filed several baseless claims in the past. He even discussed the Civil Suit that was filed years ago, citing that we're disgruntled because we lost our case. No, we're disgruntled because we've endured too many years of *"house arrest"* for opposing wrongdoing. In further attempts to intimidate and harass departmental employees, he loiters around the work area, (hands in pockets) from cubicle to cubicle, spying on his employees and listening to private conversations that are held within the cubicles. Often times, he has been observed sitting in unoccupied work stations waiting on something unforeseen to occur or be said, in attempts to report the information back to his superiors. How deceptive!

This manager has even called some employees into his office to comment and alert them that he overheard what was said. (Quite naturally, if I have the audacity to eavesdrop on someone, I wouldn't let it be known that I was snooping)! Then again, it goes back to what he said earlier, *"I do not care."* These same employees are displeased with his behavior but are afraid to voice their displeasure, fearing detrimental adverse actions when he shares their midyear or evaluative reviews. Seems to me that he is GUILTY of everything that he's been accused of and desperate to know what's being discussed in the office. To note, *"Desperate times call for desperate measures."* Simply put, his actions exude poison throughout the workplace and this same fungus has filtered over as bacteria to other levels of management abroad. The environment is "TOXIC!"

Several complaints involving Retaliatory Hostile Working Environment, Sexual Harassment, Retaliation/Reprisal, Racial/Sexual Discrimination, Working Conditions,

Evaluation/Merit Pay, Violation of Civil Rights, etc. were reported, but conditions inside remain the same. These acts are overlooked by senior executive level management officials when they are fully aware of the policy violations that are committed by their own managerial staff. Consequently, when employees seek assistance through NTEU or EEO in attempts to prevent these awfully discriminatory acts from continuing to take place, these same employees are targeted shortly thereafter, almost instantaneously.

CHAPTER XXI

My manager had a habit of calling certain employees to his office to discuss the Bible and characters in the Bible who reminds him of them. Each day, he listens to spiritual programs on the radio from 8:30 a.m. to 9:00 a.m., with intentions to be uninterrupted. If we disturb him during this period, our requests for assistance are intentionally ignored. In the alternative, if we're attempting to meet impending deadlines and refuse to loiter with him once summoned, he'll assert that we're being insubordinate. This is a miscarriage of justice.

One day he summoned me to his office and asked *"what's the shortest verse in the Bible Ms. Carter?"* I knew the answer to be *"JESUS WEPT"*. When I could not explain to him why Jesus wept, he began to openly criticize me for being ignorant. (Like he has room to talk). Due to my impending deadlines, I didn't have time to debate or rebut his comments. Finding myself somewhat befuddled, I returned to my workstation after this biblical scholar instructed me to purchase and read the New International Version (NIV), citing that this particular Bible would be better for me to comprehend so that we could discuss it later. Discuss it later? Ain't that a blip?! *(At my church, Bible Study is held on Fridays. I prefer to go there for sustenance instead of seeking absolution at work from my manager. Hallelujah)!* Again I state, my knowledge of or lack of knowledge about the Bible is not a part of my position description as a Bankruptcy Specialist. What I do know is that there should be a separation between Church, State and Federal!

One day my manager and I were conversing about a work related matter. Out of the blue he referred to me as *"Attila the Hun"*, stating that all I like to do is fight. Then he thought about what he was saying and chimed in with excitement, *"that's similar to your name spelled backwards Ms. Carter, with the exception of one "t."* What's with the name calling? I could have verbally referred to him as a *"workplace bully"* but I didn't. Oh, if he only knew what other names I wanted to spew out while he spoke. I can almost guarantee that a physical altercation would have taken place that morning. It's true when people say, *"you can dish it out, but you can't take it."* This statement overwhelmingly applies to my manager.

It's been proven, that when he's insulting an employee, he feels most comfortable. On the flip side, employees are charge with and written up for causing dissension when verbal altercations arise in the workplace. He considered that reference to be funny, as he laughed, placing his hand over his mouth. However, I was not amused and found his antics to be highly offensive. He stated that I lose every battle that I fight, so therefore *"I should be tired of going up against him!"* Why is everything a joke to this manager? Was he trying to convince himself or was he trying to convince me? His previous comment was another untruth, needless to say.

My manager is not considered a formidable adversary to say the least, after almost a decade of evaluating employees. For instance, I have been victorious in the settling of two agreements against him and his superiors regarding my annual appraisals in 2005 and 2007, respectively. For the period ending fiscal year 2005, my annual appraisal was lowered from 4.4 to 4.2, without justification, minus any written negative documentation. Each time an employee files a grievance against him in relation to an appraisal being lowered unjustifiably, ninety-nine percent of the time it's overturned in favor of the grievant. Therefore, why would anyone be *"tired of going up against him"* if they can secure a clear victory?

Despite this one revelation, my peers still refuse to solicit assistance from NTEU out of fear of reprisal. Instead, they've grown accustomed to accepting whatever ratings he feel they deserve, even if they disagree with what's documented on paper about their work ethic. This proves that evaluations are arbitrarily being lowered based on personal feelings, contrary to rules, regulations and what policy dictates.

When my evaluative appraisal covering fiscal year 2005 was shared with me by my managers' female colleague, I questioned her about the information relied on in determining my lowered numerical rating. She admitted that there was nothing negative in my personnel file to utilize in arriving at the decision to lower it. Well then if that's the case, why didn't my numerical score remain the same as the prior year, at the very least? And, why was my appraisal lowered? Almost immediately, after my persistent questioning, this individual said, *"my hands were tied, I had no other recourse."* I wanted desperately to believe her.

Matter of fact, management had not shared any documents with me (positive/negative) leading up to the rating period. You see, this goes back to what I mentioned earlier about managers not being allowed to make independent decisions. She turned *"beet red"* when I asked, *"did your boss instruct you to do this?"* Man, she did not want to implicate him or incriminate herself. She only responded by saying, *"I can't answer that."* Can't or won't? It was obvious that my questioning placed her in an awkward position. However, she has been a manager for many, many years and has been responsible for evaluating hundreds, maybe thousands of employees throughout her career. Therefore, she was fully aware that lowering my appraisal was wrong but she followed her boss' directive in doing so, I presume.

Due to my persistent nature, she advised me to file a grievance. I took her advice and did just that. Honestly, I found it odd that *"management"* would advise an employee to file a grievance. Usually, some managers make every effort to rectify the problem to prevent a grievance from being filed. After I pondered her advice, it was evident that the appraisal had been prepared by my male manager but presented to me by her. The grievance was accepted into arbitration and settled favorably in April 2007, entitling me to receive a performance award with calculated interest regarding the period in question. Things would be remiss if I failed to mention that this added fuel to the fire, giving my manager even greater cause to reprise against me. Now, who's the sore loser?

In December 2006, one of my peers became ill and was going to be out of the office for an extended period of time. After serving a twenty-five day suspension late January 2007 for having owed federal taxes, upon my return to work weeks later, I was called into my manager's office and advised that my peer's entire inventory was being assigned to me, nothing to discuss.

My one concern was that this employees' inventory consisted of several *"dogged"* cases, including ones that had been over aged for several months to many years. What's sad about this situation is that this is the same employee who was promoted years earlier, when I was denied the opportunity to interview/compete against her in the competitive selection process. Although I was responsible for my own voluminous inventory, I had no say in this reassignment. You see, to refuse management anything leads to a death sentence! Although my concerns fell on deaf ears, I did have countless concerns somewhat. My mind was playing tricks on me.

First, why wasn't this inventory reassigned to a higher graded employee? History dictates that these individuals have always had smaller inventories than anyone else in the department. Second, why wasn't the inventory assigned to others who are similarly situated? Third, why wasn't the inventory spread out amongst the workgroup as a whole? Fourth, why wasn't the group polled for suggestions as to how the inventory would be managed in this employees' absence?

As it stands, there were many variables that management could have considered regarding case resolution in this matter. None of these options were considered, that was managements' way of punishing me. Because I consider myself to be very conscientious about the work product, I applied the same diligence in working this inventory, just as I did my own. Actually, I handled her inventory with *"kid gloves"*, working late evenings every day to ensure that every deadline was met so as to remain current. However, this was a massive undertaking and challenging at best. That was one of many experiences that taught me how prayer changes things!

When my evaluation was shared with me in June 2007, my manager did not take any of my team player efforts into consideration. Better yet he stated, *"That's what's expected of you."* Why was this expected of me when my own peer was not expected to perform her required duties? This same individuals' numerical rating was 4.6 prior to leaving due to illness, whereas my numerical score was never equivalent to hers until the matter was grieved. NTEU was notified and management agreed to settle, whereas my numerical score for the period ending 2007 was raised from 4.4 to 4.6, enabling me to receive an NTEU performance award in October 2007.

Each time that I filed grievances in protest to management's wrongdoing or perhaps participated in EEO activity, I found myself lower and lower on the totem pole. It's safe to say that management doesn't like employees who exercise their rights. When this happens, you will be black-balled and retaliated against, in its ugliest form. Same as if you're attacked by a pit bull. I don't know which is worse. You'd probably fare better going heads up with the dog! In all likely possibility, that/those wounds just might heal! Despite what's been attested to by others, some wounds never heal.

Retaliation/Reprisal should be non-existent within the Service, with zero tolerance enforcements. We both know that's a joke. According to a former IRS Commissioner, *"zero tolerance is/should be the focus in these kinds of situations."* As long as I've been affiliated with the organization, I've never known anyone to be held accountable for reprising or retaliating against employees. I've witnessed and have been party to many instances of reprisal, but these devious acts committed by management are allowed to continue daily without repercussions.

More times than not, the only form of reprimand that manager's face is reassignment. Often times, the final outcome is better than positions previously held by them. Therefore, wherein does the punishment lie? That could only mean one thing: the Commissioner's policy is not being enforced. If you searched court records regarding the number of civil cases that have been filed against the Agency for this and many other various issues, the results would blow your mind!

***** **For the record, "the ones who are most familiar with the laws are the ones who violate the laws more often."** *****

SEGMENT FIVE

THE
AFTERMATH

CHAPTER XXII

Even after the untimely death of a coworker's immediate family member, management continued with their vicious attempts at harassment, angry with this employee because she prevailed against the Agency in winning her discrimination complaint. Furthermore, the individual was not afforded the opportunity to grieve the passing of her loved one. As an alternative, she had to *"feed off the sharks"* by filing complaint after complaint to refute the Agency's sabotage. For example, my manager would contact his colleagues' offsite to squeal on this employee. In doing so, his actions caused other managers to exhibit and display a biased attitude towards her, although they had never been introduced formally.

There have been many days that I've provided solace for her, allowing her to cry on my shoulders (literally) at work or home via telephone, just to help her make it through the day/night. My advice to her was, *"weeping may endure for a night, but joy cometh in the morning."* So, she wiped her tears, shook it off with a smile and was ready for the next encounter. You see, there's nothing wrong with having a good cry from time to time. It doesn't make you any less the woman/man for that matter.

Believe me, there was going to be a next encounter because management was angry at her for securing a victorious resolution to her EEO complaint. If your vision is clouded, you'll miss the surprise attack. It's coming and it's coming at you with full force! Therefore, you must have all of your *"faculties about you"* if you intend to *"go up against this organization."* Main reason, the harder you fight them, the harder the fight becomes.

Do you remember when we were young and got into fist fights with an adversary? If you got knocked down it was considered to be over. Same applies with the Agency and management, try not to get knocked down. Even if you do, gather your composure and get up quickly. Life's lesson is: *"It's not about how many times you're knocked down, it's about how fast you rise from the fall."* Why do I paint this picture of this employer? I speak from firsthand knowledge and experience. Why is it that a fight has to ensue? The Agency and management's mentality is *"bring it on!"* This attitude is exercised against employees once they complain against wrongdoing.

As far as I'm concerned, there is no such thing as *"Alternative Dispute Resolution."* If things look favorable for the employee, the Agency opts out of discussions that could possibly lead to resolution. But, if the pendulum swings in favor of the Agency, employees are expected to surrender via compromise. There is no opting out for the employee. If you refuse to cooperate, you've just purchased your one way ticket to purgatory to live out the final days as an outcast.

My manager has referred to employees in the department whom he feels could/would represent him in time of war. He specifically named one of my peers in particular, saying *"she could serve in his army because she obeys him and will do whatever he instructs her to do!"* He went further to specifically name others in the adjoining group, saying that they *"could not be on his team because they'd turn and run, leaving him on the mainline to be slaughtered."* And one other employee in that group is *"scary, spineless and has no backbone."* Actually, that's his disrespectful sentiment toward women as a whole. What does all of this have to do with the jobs we perform? His behavior has led to a disservice to the Service and to the nation's taxpayer. Time spent defending ourselves against him, takes away from precious time that could and/or should be spent resolving bankruptcy matters. After all, we are public servants.

My manager has once again referred to me as a Bible character named Uriah. Here we go again with Bible study during work hours. He *"taught"* me that *"David sent Uriah to war to be killed during battle because David coveted Uriah's wife, Bathsheba."* What was he insinuating? Is it that he's threatening to kill me if I continue to battle with him by filing EEO complaints and grievances? For the life of me, I could not ascertain the significance of this conversation. He thinks he has the ability to psychoanalyze everyone's personality, along with what they're thinking or what they may do at any given moment.

One other day, he called me into his office to advise me which Bible character fit my personality. I could tell him what character fits his personality but it wouldn't be anyone in the Bible! Fortunately for him I chose writing versus drawing. Otherwise, I'd have the perfect caricature in mind. Man, I crack myself up!

This manager often times referred to himself as King David because he considers that individual to be strong, although David made many mistakes. Was this a confession of guilt? According to scripture, *"David was a man after God's heart because he repented for his sins."* And believe me, he is no David! Moments later, he placed his head in his hands saying, " *I've made many mistakes and so has my boss, I told him that to his face."* Was he attempting to atone for his crimes? If so, he was seeking absolution from someone who was not at liberty to be open-minded. Then again, there's not enough tea in china to make me believe that he was humbling himself.

While referring to King David, he beat into his chest as if he was King Kong! It was so surreal, almost like watching the movie itself. I must admit that when his federal career ends, he should explore acting. So much for animation and self-expression. Anyone familiar with the movie knows that King Kong is a gentle giant. Oops, no comparison there. Finally, he talked about how *"David slew Goliath and how his own brothers refused to help him slay a dragon because they were afraid, so on and so on.*

My manager made this analogy referring to my cohorts saying, *"Your friends are going to abandon you too, they're weak and spineless individuals."* As if he hadn't said enough already, to make matters worse he made reference to another character in the Bible who so despised his wife, that during sexual intercourse he did not EJACULATE in her. Instead, he preferred to have his SPERM drop to the ground! Yes, his words verbatim!

There are two ways I can address these comments: First of all, I should not have been pulled away from my work to discuss the Bible and its characters that fit my personality nor his, for that matter. Second, this entire display of his sexual fantasies is NASTY! If he is intent on practicing Theology, it shouldn't be practiced at the taxpayers'/employees' expense. Unfortunately, he has appointed himself as one of God's messengers, but his actions have consistently proven to be adverse to scripture.

It's a good thing that everyone has the opportunity to get to know the Creator for themselves instead of relying on the ideas and interpretations of others. Moments later, he approached the sex topic again and attempted visual aid. I kept my eyes focused on his, refusing to follow his hands. I had just eaten lunch and did not want to regurgitate! Talk about sexual harassment. I felt embarrassed and violated as a female by his comments. This conversation was highly offensive and I reported this to a female EEO Territory Manager from Florida during questioning in another case related matter. Needless to say, this was swept under the rug also. Nothing was done.

If my manager has time to continuously summon employees into his office to converse on the Bible and its characters, when is he ever on PRODUCTION? It's been said that *"many are called, few are chosen."* In this situation, it would not have bothered me one bit to not be called or chosen. Due to health reasons, in October 2007, I was scheduled to undergo surgery and obligated to inform my manager of the six to eight week recovery period surrounding this urgent matter. Because of major complications, the surgery was postponed. When I approached his office with updated information, he asked *"will you be able to have SEXUAL INTERCOURSE with your thousand dollar man after surgery?"* Now this question really rendered me speechless because the conversation had taken on a personal flavor. OMG! I turned to leave without answering, before my knees buckled under me.......

CHAPTER XXIII

Everyone is well aware that this manager has had his share of complaints filed against him. And, if I am not mistaken, there has been more than one EEO complaint filed against him alleging sexual harassment as the claim. One might ask, *"If this person has been accused of all of these unlawful acts, why is he still in management?"* Reason being, he is the guard dog who's been allowed to lynch us and keep his paws on the throats of the more vocal African American females in the department, all the while his superiors' hands/paws are free from scrutiny.

This is the only conclusion that's clear to me. Surely, it's not due to his qualifications and/or job knowledge. However, an allegation is just that until proven otherwise. I believe in a person's innocence until proven guilty. That's what's called due diligence. But, what has been the outcome once an employee's guilt surfaced? For managers, retribution. For employees, removal. However, I guess everyone feels secure when their *"guard dog"* is on the prowl. Woof........

There are Hispanic employees in the department who's allowed to STEAL credit hours daily with no repercussions, opting to remain in the office until almost midnight, pretending to be working, when in fact this constitutes a contract violation and a safety issue. If memory serves me correctly, the computer system is inoperable after a certain hour in the evening. Therefore, I'm left asking a question that should have been initiated by management years earlier. *"What could you possibly be working on that's so important it can't wait until the next day?"* Management is aware of what's going on because they are responsible for signing the timesheets. What's flabbergasting is that I've called very late nights and the employee had the audacity to answer the phone! Surely she didn't expect customers to call the office after 9:00 p.m., same applies to other creditors. Furthermore, she should not have been there to answer!

On the flip side, there's a male Caucasian employee in the department who's allowed to work at a different satellite office most days, because he has openly voiced to management that *"he does not like working with certain employees in the office"*, all the while he's assigned a smaller caseload as incentive. This revelation in and of itself is malevolent and should not have gone unchecked. In the interim, there are other fringe benefits afforded him. For example, when employees travel to other offices, they submit travel vouchers for managerial approval as a form of payback, then they're paid per diem for miles traveled.

Although costly for the Agency, it's profitable for the employee. This GS 11's exorbitant, fraudulent travel vouchers are approved without questioning, while others' exploits are examined under a microscope. Anyway, it has been said that he spends the majority of government time visiting his *"significant other"* while in travel status. How interesting. Nevertheless, this practice has been approved for many years by our group manager, this employees' former manager, and questioned by acting managers in the department, territory wide. It must be a really, really good feeling to be the recipient of so many CARTE BLANCHE privileges. For these reasons and more, my manager's actions constitute an unlawful abuse of policy. This is something that TIGTA should be researching instead of harassing employees via secret investigations!

It has been an accepted, common practice for individuals to congregate in my manager's office, talking down and belittling certain employees who are despised by management, all the while everyone's being paid for production. I can say these things with certainty because I've witnessed the occurrences too often. Furthermore, it doesn't take a rocket scientist to ascertain which employees are being discussed. Once everyone exits his office, they actually have the audacity to laugh out loud, in the presence of others who have gathered. What I find to be funny is, the ones who congregate in his office are the *"non-performers."* This is also a known, proven fact. Obviously, he sees himself in them. Oops, I went and did it again!

This manager talks openly about employees in the work area, naming each one whom he feels know their jobs versus those who are less skilled. If they only knew what he thinks about them. You already know what he thinks about me. *"Why am I still the topic of discussion after so much time has passed?"* Did I leave that much of an impression upon him? I hope so. It is also my hope that *"whenever he sees my name, every unkind word spoken, every unkind deed acted upon and every atrocious and heinous act committed, take center stage in his mind."*

On an outstanding grading scale of 5.0, it's been stated that my manager received a 3.0 (fully successful) from his manager, prior to being appointed to a temporary managerial position in Insolvency. To exert his authority, he began a vicious campaign against certain individuals, by lowering their appraisals, without written negative documentation as proof. Because of his amoral acts, some employees quit their jobs and some opted to retire earlier than anticipated in attempts to escape this manager's TYRANNY! For example, in December 2007, a GS 1169-12 Revenue Officer/Advisor retired after thirty years of service with the IRS. No details were forthcoming surrounding his abrupt decision to retire.

In February (same year), my manager was out of the office for about three (3) months due to an illness that required surgery. In his absence, a manager from the Phoenix office served in his stead, someone that supposedly was a close friend of his. From the onset, she proved to be one of the most professional supervisors I've had the pleasure to work for in a very long time. The entire group formed a professional relationship with her and quite frankly did not want her detail to end. She was a breath of fresh air! During her assignment in Houston, she attempted to balance the inventories between the employees, no matter the grade level. I respected that about her.

However, when our manager got wind of what was going on, he called from his hospital bed, speaking with certain employees in the group, voicing his displeasure. Upon his return to work weeks/months later, he verbally reprimanded us, accusing us of liking her too much and going along with the changes she made in his absence without his consent. He called me into the office and let loose on me, stating *"Alita, I'm really surprised at you!"* *What did he expect?* She had the authority to delegate whatever changes she deemed necessary. This manager did not need his consent. He was on sick leave and therefore had no authority. That's why someone was appointed to act for him. Duh!

I guess he expected his employees to balk and complain openly to her, and to display a level of defiance by giving her a hard time. Since none of these things occurred, he was absolutely furious with several of us. Better yet, when she advised him that everything went smoothly, that really angered him for about three additional months. Mainly because he has advised other levels of management that the Houston employees conduct themselves like characters on the *"Wild, Wild West"*. Since nothing out of the ordinary took place, his negative comments lacked credence.

Days later, I witnessed my manager sitting in an employee's cubicle for many, many hours on end, expressing discontent about this female colleague from Phoenix, stating that *"he was tired of hearing his employees mention her name."* This is a prime example why things are the way they are in Houston because my manager has contributed to and on many, many occasions created the Hostile Work Environment single-handedly with the go ahead green light received from executive level management.

Because of my close association with my former male manager, my current mal manager thought it necessary to inform me that the reason my friend retired when he did is because *"he was forced out due to the number of barred statute cases that his revenue officer group was responsible for"*. He said that *"had this individual not retired, he would have endured years of sheer terror from his superiors."* As previously stated, I don't understand my manager's lack of loyalty to colleagues.

Prior to my former manager's retirement, my manager would contact him on several occasions for moral support. And, he was not refused assistance. Matter of fact, when my friend was a manager in SPB for almost two years, there were no complaints or grievances filed and the climate was not HOSTILE! Actually, we looked forward to returning to work the following day. Can this manager say the same? Yes, his comments angered me. That was his intent. Again, I had to display a poker face and that was extremely difficult. I wanted desperately to make him *"eat"* those words, if you know what I mean!

By the time my manager served in the department in his acting capacity from October 2001 through December 2004, he and his superiors had already been the recipients of at least four to five complaints alleging what else, DISCRIMINATION! This individual's permanent status as manager did not officially begin until January 2005, whereas since that time period alone, he has incurred even more. This is not good. I don't think he has room to talk does he? Just recently, he angrily commented to three employees *"I'm going to set you HEIFER'S straight!"* Heifers? How rude and unprofessional! The workplace is no place for these repeated insults and lack of respect by management. In the alternative, had this comment been directed towards a manager, the employee(s) would have been severely disciplined. Nevertheless, my manager has not suffered any form of adverse action for his behavior unbecoming a manager, although the comment was documented and grieved by NTEU.

In the final analysis, this manager mentioned his unsolicited, awful sentiments to me in order to tarnish my friend's character because he was aware of our status. Anything this individual mentions to me about him did not/has not tarnished my feelings. I say this adamantly because my former manager has been placed in situations where he felt compelled to defend me. You see, that's what true friends do. If my current manager had any true friends, he'd understand exactly what I mean. Although his intent failed, his actions are not to be excused! *"With the exception of honor, loyalty governs."* This is a quote to live by and we all should practice this in our everyday dealings with one another.

CHAPTER XXIV

On June 5, 2007, I received a call from my manager summoning me to his office, as he passed a note with directions for me to contact TIGTA as soon as possible. I was under investigation for "misuse" of computer e-mail, allegedly for transmitting them in violation of policy. Isn't that a riot? Nevertheless, I wasn't worried one bit—thinking that everyone in the department would be facing the same scrutiny.

Each of us at one time or another, transmit e-mails on a daily basis, across the IRS spectrum and abroad, to internal/external customers, friends and family, knowingly/willingly, regardless of any *"supposed"* policy violations. However, only four employees within my department were summoned for questioning and interviewed about this infraction. During the meeting, I was advised that my transmissions were not as egregious as others. Far be it from that, having admitted to doing this was a determining factor in the end—TERMINATION.

Upon meeting with the agent the following day, only one e-mail was called into play, one that I remembered right away. According to the TIGTA agent, an employee was offended by its discriminant nature, as to why I was being questioned. There were thirteen specifications in total, encompassing the timelines from December 15, 2005 - June 21, 2006. Is it the Agency's contention that there were no e-mail transmissions subsequent this time? I beg to differ. I received so many e-mail transmissions from employees, sometimes they remained unopened. Now, as soon as I decide to transmit one, a siren goes off! As I attested to during questioning, what about the individuals who transmitted e-mails to me on a consistent basis. What form of punishment did they suffer, if any?

For instance, one e-mail that was transmitted to me from another employee on April 3, 2006, was also transmitted to twenty three employees; another one that was transmitted to me on June 20, 2006, was transmitted to fourteen employees; and lastly, one that was transmitted to me on June 15, 2006 was sent to fifteen others, etc. Now, you should see where I'm going with this analysis. Again I state, I have never created any e-mails, jokes or chain letters. Furthermore, the TIGTA agent advised me that my investigation was a "spinoff" from another case involving an employee in the adjoining group. Yeah right. Obviously, this was another lie!

As it stands, I distinctly recall this employee's computer being confiscated for *"alleged pornography"*, calling into play any other e-mails that were deemed obscene or offensive. However, I didn't think things were intertwined. The periods of investigation covered February 28, 2007-June 6, 2007. Two weeks after returning to duty off suspension, this investigation was birthed. However, a coworker and NTEU had recently received a *"favorable"* arbitration ruling days earlier against the Agency along this same time period, and I gave sworn testimony in support of her. Guess what else? My civil lawsuit against the Agency was dismissed in June 2007. Coincidence? No way!

On August 20, 2007, the Territory Manager requested a meeting with the EEO Territory Manager, as well as with Labor Relations, to discuss the *"Houston"* employees and what type of punishment they should be subjected to. Two days later, my employee transcript was requested and routed to management via expedite. One week subsequent that request, a teleconference was held with my Territory Manager, the *"incoming"* Area Manager, two Labor Relations officials, the EEO Territory Manager from Florida and two of the Agency attorneys. As a result of owing federal taxes for the period ending 2006, my account was assigned to a field officer for enforced collection in September 2007. A grand scheme. Matter of fact, the Area Manager would not be serving in her new role until fiscal 2008, which was to begin in October 2007. Why was she being briefed months earlier? And, what was her involvement prior to assuming her new role?

EEO? Excuse me. I thought that EEO's role was a neutral one. If so, why is this EEO Territory Manager conversing with the Agency attorneys and senior level executive officials via e-mail and conference calls, addressing matters with intent to *"bring down"* certain employees in the Houston office whom management despised? This, once again is unethical and detrimental to employee careers.

These acts must be addressed and dealt with accordingly. Otherwise, the problems will continue to fester, as have been the case for years. For the record, *"when EEO is in bed with the Agency, it is awfully difficult for employees to prevail administratively once discrimination complaints are filed."*

However, this same EEO Territory Manager visited the Houston office sometime in 2006, speaking with several employees individually, in the EEO conference room about the *"goings on"* in the office, supposedly to help remedy matters concerning employee dissatisfaction with management, based on the number of claims that have been filed here. This was a ploy also.

This individual identified herself saying, *"I'm here on the behalf of the Commissioner's office."* She further advised us saying, *"I'm preparing a report for the Commissioner, but the employees will not be "privy" to its findings."* We were all pleased because we thought that help was on the way! *"It's about time we all thought—finally we'd get the attention the office deserved."* On the contrary, things spiraled out of control immediately. When this EEO Manager was questioned about the report weeks to months later, her exact words were *"I lost it."* Yeah right! We were set up! I'll bet the Commissioner was unaware of her visit. Regardless of what she professed to, someone somewhere has a copy. Just because information is deleted from the computer, it's can be retrieved from a hard drive. To note, it's never really lost. Food for thought.........

On October 4, 2007, I was summoned into my manager's office and presented with the Agency's Notice of Proposal for infractions that I feel I should not have been held accountable for. I'm not totally innocent and have accepted partial responsibility. As I entered his office, I noticed that he looked disturbed, holding his head as if he was in engrossed in deep thought. He seemed awfully sad and forlorn, seeking sympathy. When I attempted to discuss the matter with him, to my surprise he was responsive and willingly approached the subject that I deemed most urgent. For a moment there, it almost felt as if he cared. On this day, he acted the way I'd expect a good manager would. I'm sure he felt awkward addressing me because he knew all along that the Agency's proposal would be unfavorable, based on HIS recommendation as my first-line manager. But, I'm not supposed to know protocol.

After leaving my manager's office, I read the document at my desk several times, pondering my next step. Well, since this was about me, who better to respond to the Agency's proposal other than myself. As it stands, I disregarded my own advice, *"never commit it to paper."*

Yes, I submitted my version of why I was in that predicament, hoping that it proved useful. Only time would tell. Not that I didn't trust anyone else to intercede for me, actually I didn't believe that things were as serious as they appeared. Silly me. For weeks I walked around in oblivion, not knowing when or if the hammer was going to drop for the final time. In all honesty, that's not a good feeling. It was absolutely hard for me to come to work subsequent that time and be expected to perform as if everything was fine.

Just like the next person, I *"faked and shaked"* from the beginning of the tour until my tour ended, whereas my coworkers, friends and peer group were none the wiser. Truth be told, they had absolutely no idea what I was experiencing internally. Why burden them? Everyone has their fair share of their own problems. Who wants to hear mine? However, I looked forward to each day being a new day.

Initially, when I received the Agency's proposal letter, my manager had the audacity to ask " *is this the root cause of your bouts with high blood pressure?"* By the way, the Agency's proposal was to remove me OR otherwise discipline me, decision to be forthcoming within thirty days. My manager referred to the suspension in 1995 as my first offense, my suspension in January 2007 as my second offense and this infraction a third offense. I explained that the first offense is barred by statute because it occurred over twelve years prior to. Therefore, "progressive discipline" was not applied accordingly.

The last offense included *"misuse of computer e-mail for failure to protect my government issued computer", as it relates to "Security" under Critical Element-(4E) Business Results/Quality."* If I failed to protect my computer, why then have I received "Outstanding" in this same aspect year after year, specifically for the periods ending 2005 and 2007, respectively? If their assertion was valid, a rational person would assume that I've **"Failed"** in that aspect, after having received negative documentation from management during the rating period. There was none. Allow me to say this, I have never received anything less than Exceeds Fully Successful in this area time and time again.

As we conversed about the subject matter, my manager looked up at me with *"puppy dog eyes"*, immediately stating *"the decision was not mine. I had no input whatsoever."* I was dumbfounded, for lack of a better word. For the simple reason, the Discrimination complaint that I filed in September 2005 was still ongoing when management took the adverse action against me surrounding the suspension in January 2007, in violation of my Title VII rights, which is discriminatory also.

Although I knew that his comment was untrue, I did not let on that I knew otherwise. For the record, anytime an employee is subjected to a proposed adverse action, the employees' first line manager is questioned about appropriate disciplinary actions. After having researched the matter myself, I find that according to Article 39 (Adverse Actions) Section 9 of the National Agreement, it states: *"supervisors are responsible for determining the type of penalty to initiate for alleged conduct violations.* Therefore, it has always been my contention that the recommendation to terminate was initiated by my manager. If I'm wrong, I'll eat glass.

When he inquired about my blood pressure, I almost passed out! He knows that my pressure problems became more prevalent when he began his crusade to violate and trample on my civil rights, as early as 2002, when the initial EEO complaint was filed. Things escalated when the Agency willfully and intentionally disallowed me the opportunity to compete and interview for a promotion within my department during this same period. As if he really cares about me or my blood pressure! The Agency displayed a lack of regard for my interests and qualifications in this position. Therefore, no one will ever know exactly what profound affect all of this had on my psyche.

I could attempt to explain to you how I feel but you wouldn't understand unless you walked a mile in my shoes.

The experience wasn't all bad, out of it another individual evolved. Now I savor every moment, taking pride in the intangible gifts I possess, not taking things for granted any longer, it can all be gone in the blink of an eye. Believe it or not, I've learned to do more with less. I'm a SURVIVOR whose heart is filled with PRAISE. People seem to think that I'm really strong because of the image I portray. In actuality, I'm probably the most sensitive individual you'll ever meet. I'm not ashamed to admit this one revelation. Life's lessons have taught me that sensitive individuals are good hearted individuals. And, I've been introduced to a few in my lifetime. If you allow people to know what hurts you, they'll bruise your psyche. No one likes to be hurt.

Unfortunately, I believed in my employer to the point that I let my guard down. In the final analysis, I became someone that I didn't even like. Never once did I say *"why me"* or allow myself to wallow in self-pity. But, I often wondered why my career was altered permanently, from a twenty five day suspension to removal. In spite of this, I was able to give *"birth"* to my dream. I'm living my ultimate dream each time a word, phrase or anecdote leaps from these pages—into the hearts and minds of others. No more burdens—my shackles are broken. It wasn't until months later when it was all revealed to me. I didn't face my personal demons earlier on, refusing to acknowledge what was happening. In actuality, I now believe that *"things happen for you, not to you." Having said that, our darkest days can bring about many, many wonderful things into our lives. Be strong and of good courage, the Lord your God is with you. Joshua 1:9*

Prior to giving sworn testimony on November 8, 2007, in support of a coworker's EEO allegations against management, I'd conversed with an EEO Counselor via e-mail surrounding allegations of discrimination by management. Days earlier, my manager angrily insisted via telephone that I come into his office. As soon as I entered, he threatened me by saying, *"maybe you should reconsider involvement in this process because you have people looking at you now and things don't look good."* It was all a conspiracy! What's ironic is that prior to giving sworn testimony in this case, I was also a witness days earlier in another coworker's EEO complaint, same issues and claims. If this is not reprisal, I do not know what is.

Needless to say, six days after exercising my protected rights, I received the Agency's Notice of Removal. The effective date was November 16, 2007. My manager said, *"Strike three you're out! You've got to go Alita. I'm not sure you can be rehabilitated."* Rehabilitated? That's a joke. Goes to show exactly what my employer thought of me. I wasn't even given thirty days to clear out nor was consideration given in regards to the upcoming holiday season. Management wanted me gone at all costs. Looking at their record, coupled with all of their *"documented injustices"*, I was the liability. Imagine that.

My manager remarked that this action was harsh. As we discussed the Agency's decision, he looked puzzled and did not understand the peaceful calm on my face nor the calmness in my voice. *"Oh, ye of little faith."* Do you remember earlier on when I mentioned that my steps were ordered by God? Well, if HE ordered my steps, then that means HE prepared me for that exact moment. With that being said, *"Whom shall I fear?"* The LORD is the strength of my life, whom shall I fear? It's always good to keep them guessing! All is well with my soul. Some others cannot honestly admit the same.

"This peace that I have, the world didn't give it, the world can't take it away. Often times than not, we have no control over WHAT happens to us. However, we can control HOW we handle what happens to us. The one thing you can't take away from me is the way I choose to respond to what you do to me. Lastly, my one freedom is to choose my attitude in any given situation." My niece has always exclaimed that a person's attitude determines their altitude. Enough said....

After conversing with my manager about this delicate matter, I then sought assistance from NTEU, speaking with the Vice President as she prepared to leave the conference room, after attending another groups' meeting. I passed the document to her, she read it silently and responded. But, her response was one I hadn't expected. She said, *"There's nothing that NTEU can do for you because you responded to the issue on your own, without seeking assistance from us earlier on when you received the proposal letter."* I was awestruck. Then I asked *"is the Agency justified in saying that the suspension I served in 1995 qualifies as my first offense, although the infraction occurred twelve years prior to?"* Her response was *"yes, they can use that against you."* In my mind I'm saying, *"I know they'll try to do that but does that make it right?* I said, *"what about statute, doesn't statute matter?"* She had no response but agreed to research the question for me as she turned to leave, only after wishing me *"good luck"* in the future.

Then and only then did I realize that things would never be the same again. I've always been told that *"nothing beats a failure but a try."* No finger was lifted to help me. Often times I've asked myself *"why did I pay Union dues for so many years, if I can't see the benefit from this entity that's in place to protect the rights of its members?* Moot point now, but something for others similarly situated to ponder for future reference.

Without a doubt, I strongly believe that this very severe adverse action was taken against me because of my affiliation with certain employees, as well as for my participation in prior protected class EEO activity, as a complainant and witness. This is discriminatory. Look at the timeline. To have this happen is a violation of policy and is unlawful.   If you take into consideration the timeframes of occurrences, you'll clearly see that a connection has taken place, leading to inference.

As I prepared to undergo the clearance process with my manager two days later, he said *"girl, you have entirely too much power! You don't realize exactly how much power you have."* At that moment, I knew I was expendable, not that I wasn't aware of that one fact earlier on.

Before leaving his office he said, *"You'll be alright Alita. You can get your monies from your retirement."* Who has that mindset when their career is abruptly ending? In his mind, he actually thought he was being helpful. Or had the sarcasm resurfaced as usual? For some strange reason, he felt the need to advise me once more saying, *"After you're gone, they'll get along just fine, and they'll be forced to. Everyone is vying for attention from you."* Any time he witnessed coworkers coming to my work area, he would leave his office and come to my desk in attempts to get them to retreat.

Afterwards, he would call me into his office and demand that they be advised (once again) to stay away from his work area. As previously stated, I am the only individual this request applied to. Several of my coworkers had visitors daily, some employees sat for hours in his presence, etc. but nothing was ever addressed to them.

If my visitors did not leave when he felt they should, he would intentionally search for excuses to come to my work area, as a form of intimidation, sometimes standing there until the employee(s) left. This blatant and reprehensible tactic is widespread within this organization. *"He does not fear bad news, or live in dread of what may happen. For he is settled in his mind that Jehovah will take care of him. That is why he is not afraid but can calmly face his foes. He gives generously to those in need. His deed will never be forgotten. He shall have influence and honor. Evil minded men will be infuriated when they see all this, they will gnash their teeth in anger and slink away, their hopes thwarted."* Psalms 112:7-10

CHAPTER XXV

When I was summoned to my manager's office to undergo clearance, he advised me that he was tempted to purchase a taped cassette for me from his church because the Pastor's message reminded him of the dilemma that I was about to face. Instinctively, he decided against purchasing the cassette after exercising better judgment. I stood there flabbergasted, not being able to speak out of sheer shock! He mentioned to me that he had come to grips with the Agency's decision, stating that *"he was upset with me for leaving him."* For the record, I did not leave him, I left the Service.

Moments later he said, *"I only have one employee in this group who's almost on your level, as far as job performance. I have begun to take her under my wings."* cause my expression, but Oh Lord! Although I could have emphatically stated that *"no one's performance in his group could compare to my own"*, I remained silent and continued to listen to his condescending revelations.

I thought it odd for him to verbalize laudatory comments about my work ethics when in fact he'd lower my performance evaluations every other year (without provocation), based on his personal feelings and not what the policy, rules and regulations dictate.

Days after separating, in attempts to further exacerbate the situation, it was stated that my former manager approached several employees in the workgroup, voiced many unsavory comments about me as well as asking, *"What do you all think of Alita's departure? How many of you are glad that she's gone?"* His unprofessional, unethical badgering alone violates EEO laws regarding POST SEPARATION and is DISCRIMINATORY! It was also stated that some of my peers admitted that they were glad that I'm gone. Always remember, *"If he talks about me to you, who is he talking to about you?"*

Adding fuel to the fire in attempts to disparage me, he conducted a stand-up meeting to advise my peers *"not to speak with me"* in the event that I called the office, as well as instructing them to alert him if/when I called. What was his intent? Heaven only knows. And, he advised the workgroup that I wasn't even welcomed in the building, with the exception of visiting NTEU or the Credit Union if the need arose. Oh now, he's on security detail. What gives him the right to sit in judgment by monitoring my steps, after the awfully discriminatory violations that he and his superiors willfully and intentionally commit daily? If you ask me, each of them needs a wardrobe change. How about orange? Better yet, they may look better in black and white stripes!

Having said that, the only thing about all of this that troubled me is that my so-called peer group honors his dastardly demands to date. It would not have been outside the norm for me to dial someone's number, after having worked with them throughout my IRS career. Once I was advised of these things, I refrained from calling so as to spare them from him. What prevented them from calling me though? It's funny. People are so quick to forget what's done for them. The good thing is, God never forgets. Despite that, I do believe that the world is full of good people. In actuality, no one really knows anyone. As a result, life is filled with surprises.

Ironically, many times I found myself defending these same individuals against comments this management official stated about them, only to have him reprise against me for speaking out. No, I wasn't acting as an advocate or spokesperson for the group—I wouldn't be me if I stood by and said nothing. Common sense dictates that if a person witnesses something, they should say something. For years I dealt with management's insensitivity the best way I saw fit, until which time their hurtful, deceitful words almost consumed me like a raging fire. *"One day I looked around and those same things didn't matter anymore. I matter."*

Unfortunately, this is the same peer group who turned a deaf ear in defense of management. Some of you should remember what I said years ago, *"me today, you tomorrow."* Now, after all of these years, the pendulum continues to swing out of control! I can only address this by saying *"as long as management has the ability to conceal true crime from the powers that be in National Office, my manager and his superiors will continue to reign free, exerting dominance and control over matters that are already almost beyond repair."* Hopefully, after reading these pages, his and others status as manager, executive and senior executive level, will come to an abrupt ending. This will be what's called *"TRUE JUSTICE!"* Hmm, should this be the title of my next book?

CHAPTER XXVI

As I cleared things away that dreadful day, it felt as if I was signing my life away. For it took many days and months for me to realize that God enlarges our territories by moving us from our current surroundings so that our dreams can come to fruition. Otherwise, a dream would never be more than just that. Never think that your dreams are too small or too big. The concept is to have a dream and watch it materialize. I dare each of you to dream.

According to the plan that God has for all of our lives, he can and will turn our obstacles into victories, after it's all said and done. I feel confident that God has something spectacular in store for me and I'm excited to see rainbow's end. A person's past does not have to define their future. My future is promising, for my brightest days are before me. I am the Master of my fate. When no one else believed, I pressed toward the mark all by my lonesome, refusing to let my dream die. Simply put, I've always believed in my ability to overcome pitfalls. However, sometimes I can be my own worst enemy. My dream was so powerful it chased me down and overtook me. As it stands, the moment it happened I could not deny the inevitable any longer. Fate was calling. Rightfully so, I answered.

Since you are near the very end, you're probably saying *"be careful what you tell Alita, you just might see it in print."* To note, if confidentiality had been a requirement, none of most of what you've read would have been revealed. These comments were disclosed as a result of the many unsolicited conversations held with management. For the record, the reason why things have ridiculously ballooned out of control in federal government is because some are under the impression that if they remain silent, the problems that exist will magically disappear. Several employees in the department are absolutely miserable and literally exasperated, reporting to work daily facing the absurd managerial expectations to perform under dire straits. These employees are actually trying to cope, anticipating retirement by counting down the years until they can say ADIOS to the IRS.

In the meantime, some are content to accept whatever BONES that's thrown in their direction, even when they see the winds of change about to overtake them. But, what if by chance you don't make it to retirement? As we all know, this manager and his superiors are patiently waiting to throw some of you out the same way trash is disposed of. Remember what he said years ago, *"I'm not going down by myself!"* At the time the comment was expressed verbally, I didn't understand why he'd say something of that nature. Oh, but now I fully understand its ramifications.

Because of the ongoing acts of malfeasance committed abroad, ONE problem has become TWO, TWO has become THREE, and so on. The damages that have been done are infinite and limitless. How will anyone know that problems exist if the employees are expected to remain *"close mouthed"* so that management can continuously sweep injustices under the rug as have been the case for decades?

To some managers, the employees do not matter one iota. Despite this, there comes a time in all of our lives when we must take a stand and demand what's rightfully ours. Why is it that when female employees defend themselves against management, they're stereotyped as *"angry Black women?"* For the record, not all women are angry. Better yet, not all angry women are Black! The real reason has not been explored to date. I declare, *"It's the "weak male" who can't deal with some female personalities from the onset."*

To have the pleasure of working in environments that are FREE from Retaliation/Reprisal, Harassment, Discrimination, etc., is to be expected, according to the policies, rules and regulations set forth by established law. Second, being treated with DIGNITY and RESPECT daily wouldn't reside outside the realm of normality. Just think how AWESOME the workplace would be if policy was consistently adhered to.

Although the Agency's malicious intent and actions caused a disparate impact in the terms and conditions of my employment in 2002 and subsequent that time, I accept that promotions come from God not man. Often times than not, what the DEVIL meant for bad works to a person's advantage. And just like the boomerang, what goes around comes around. I've learned how not to look upon adversity as something bad, often times it can be opportunity in disguise.

After all of the adversity that's come my way, this was the Agency's *"last ditch effort"* to break me down. Guess what? Even this strategy didn't work! It's been said that *"Whatever doesn't kill you makes you stronger."* This experience has done just that. I'm still standing TALL, ready to face the next chapter in my life. In closing, I unequivocally believe that if we continue to practice patience by waiting on God, one day real soon *"JUSTICE WILL PREVAIL."* This is my dream. *"Now glory be to God who by his mighty power at work within us is able to do far more than we would ever dare to ask or even dream of-infinitely beyond our highest prayers, desires, thoughts or hopes."*

Ephesians 3:20

EPILOGUE

I've often wondered what this world would be like if there were no laws or rules set forth to govern its existence. Many prominent individuals have lost their lives exercising privileges afforded us via the Constitution. To live in a country free from tyrannical rule is comforting. However, to live in this great country and be treated as if you're from a third-world nation where leaders run "roughshod" over citizens with no repercussions on the horizon is unjust. Some employees within federal government operate by the aforementioned, profane standards. Sadly so, they consider their insidious actions to be above reproach and without consequence, having met the expected and accepted organizational objectives through coercion, restraint, interference, etc.

In certain instances when subordinates are oppressed, often times managerial staff officials are the recipients of rewards via promotion and increase. Remember, abuse does not only have to be physical to cause irreparable damage. I declare, *"there are no hierarchies in a Democratic society...we all are each other's equal."* Despite this, the Agency enjoys its consistent game of *"cat and mouse"*, playing musical chairs with employees' livelihoods and careers. This common practice is unacceptable and must be abolished.

No man or woman is exempt from carrying out the intended purpose of the government's mandated policy. And, when things go awry or attempts are initiated to willfully and intentionally circumvent policy regulations, what's left is accountability, utilizing the appropriate guidelines...regardless of one's status and position within said organization. In other words, when the Agency is slow to take action, or resign themselves to take no action when faced with documented injustices against its staff, culpability exists. As a result, when evil is allowed to go unchecked, the command or go ahead has been authorized by higher ups. Almost always.

To be an *"asset of change"*, IRS administration must be vigilant by not only *"lending an ear"* to the plight of its employees, it must also be prepared to make certain that only the *"best and brightest"* employees/managers at all levels, are at its fore font, protecting and serving in the government's best interest. Otherwise, the system will continue to crumble via meltdown. Employees should be any organizations' greatest asset. With certainty, the mind of an employee is his/her greatest asset.

Placing a bandage on the sore is not treating the wound, it's only covering up the existing problem. If getting the word out this way has been instrumental at all, then I will have made an impact in my lifetime. Now, I'm free to *"spread my wings and soar above the limitations that had me bound."* It has been said that one person can make a difference. If I'm that one person, **MISSION ACCOMPLISHED**. And, I still believe in happy endings. *TO BE CONTINUED!!!!!*

"But they that wait upon the Lord shall renew their strength; they shall mount up with wings as eagles; they shall run and not be weary; and they shall walk and not faint." Isaiah 40:31

THE END

BIOGRAPHY

Alita Carter is a former Chapter 13 Bankruptcy Specialist with twenty four years of dedicated service to the Internal Revenue Service. This is her first manuscript. She's currently enrolled in school with aspirations of becoming a freelance writer/published author.

After being diagnosed with Colon Cancer in 2009, after two successful surgeries and six months of chemotherapy, her condition is stable as of the writing of this book. Because of God's Grace and Mercy, Alita Carter is a Cancer survivor whose heart is filled with praise.

She has one son and one daughter. Aside from reading, writing, shopping and traveling, her passion is spending quality time with her three grandchildren. Alita Carter is single and resides in Houston with family.

WHEN WILL JUSTICE PREVAIL?

ALITA CARTER HAS SPOKEN THE TRUTH TO POWER, AND AS A RESULT, ALL IS RIGHT WITH HER SOUL. SHE HAS FOUGHT THE GOOD FIGHT AGAINST EVIL, TAKEN ITS BEST SHOT, AND MORE IMPORTANTLY, SHE KNOWS THAT GOD, THE HEAVENLY FATHER, THE HOLY SPIRIT AND HER LORD AND PERSONAL SAVIOR, JESUS CHRIST, ARE IN CONTROL.

NO WEAPON FORMED AGAINST MS. CARTER WILL PROSPER. AND WHILE ALL INDEED IS WELL WITH HER SOUL, SHE WANTS THE WORLD TO KNOW THE EVIL THAT MEN DO WHEN THEY ARE GIVEN UNCHECKED POWER. HOPEFULLY THE WORLD WILL LEARN FROM HER STORY ABOUT THE BIG BAD BULLY CALLED THE IRS. MS. CARTER IS TRULY COURAGOUS. HER STORY IS AN INSPIRATION TO ALL AND SHOULD BE APPLAUDED.

WHEN WILL

JUSTICE

PREVAIL

AN INSIDER'S VIEW BY
FORMER IRS EMPLOYEE

ALITA CARTER

ALITA CARTER'S SENSATIONAL BOOK

WHEN WILL JUSTICE PREVAIL?

AN INSIDER'S VIEW BY A FORMER IRS EMPLOYEE

The Internal Revenue Service:
Acts of Malfeasance, Malevolence and Malice Revealed

ZWORLDNET
PUBLISHING
INC.

THE AWESOME
POWER

OF THE

WRITTEN
WORD!

WWW.ZWORLDNET.COM

WHEN WILL JUSTICE PREVAIL?
By
ALITA CARTER

PUBLISHED BY ZWORLDNET PUBLISHING INC.
ISBN 978-09712310-6-1 / WWW.ZWORLDNET.COM

**I FEAR NO EVIL
BECAUSE I KNOW MY GOD IS IN CONTROL,
LOVES TRUTH AND JUSTICE, IS ALWAYS
WITH ME AND WILL VANQUISH ALL WHO DEFY
MY RIGHTEOUSNESS AND TRUTH!!!**

**AND SO, THEREFORE, I WILL NOT BE SILENT!
I WILL SHOUT TO THE WORLD! TO GOD BE
THE VICTORY AND GLORY! AND MAY THAT
TRUTH THAT I HAVE FOUGHT FOR WITH MY
BLOOD AND TEARS AND BROUGHT INTO THE
LIGHT, LINGER MIGHTILY
AND SHAKE THIS WORLD LONG AFTER I AM
GONE FROM THIS EARTH!!!!**

It has been said that one person can make a difference. If I'm
that one person, **MISSION ACCOMPLISHED!**

ALITA CARTER

WHEN WILL JUSTICE REVAIL?

PUBLISHED BY ZWORLDNET PUBLISHING INC.
ISBN 978-09712310-6-1
THIS BOOK AND ALL OTHER ZWORLDNET PUBLISHING
BOOKS CAN BE PURCHASED AT WWW.ZWORLDNET.COM

www.ingramcontent.com/pod-product-compliance
Lightning Source LLC
Chambersburg PA
CBHW021539260326
41914CB00001B/81